Praise for *SHIFTS*

"Dr. Sam Adeyemi has proven himself as a reliable voice in transformational leadership and a true catalyst for change. This book is a valuable resource for anyone ready to shift their mindset and rise to the next level in leadership. A worthy investment of your time and energy!"

—Ibukun Awosika
entrepreneur, author, and thought leader; former chairman, First Bank of Nigeria PLC; founder and CEO, The Chair Centre Group

"Considering that most transformation programs fail in organizations, in this book, Sam provides a practical framework, SHIFT, that every leader can use to achieve desired outcomes from their transformation programs."

—Olu Adegoke
global managing partner, Communications, Media and Technology Practice, Infosys Consulting

"*SHIFTS* is not just a guide to mindset transformation; it's a deeply personal journey brought to life by Sam's own remarkable experiences. Sam's personal stories inspire readers to embrace these powerful mindset shifts in their own lives, offering practical tools to lead with vision, resilience, and purpose."

—Drew Gerber
CEO, Wasabi Publicity, Inc.

"*SHIFTS* offers tools to navigate these changes with grace, turning challenges into opportunities for growth. It's a must-read for anyone who wants to lead with heart and purpose."

—Ken Honda
Zen millionaire, bestselling author of *Happy Money*

"Dr. Adeyemi understands that true leadership is not just about achieving success but also creating positive change that elevates everyone. This book is an inspiring road map for leaders ready to embrace a more expansive, heart-centered approach to leadership and leave a lasting impact on the world."

—Steve Farrell
cofounder and worldwide executive director of Humanity's team, author of *A New Universal Dream*

"This book not only equips readers with practical tools but also inspires a transformative mindset that is crucial in today's complex landscape. *SHIFTS* is a must-read for anyone dedicated to leading with integrity and purpose."

—Portia Wood
founder of Wood Legal Group, LLP;
generational wealth expert

"*SHIFTS* is a pivotal read for leaders who want to cultivate not only external success but also internal depth and fulfillment."

—Kirk J. Schneider, PhD
psychologist, 2022 candidate for president of the American Psychological Association (APA), author

"*SHIFTS* is a profound guide that speaks directly to the evolving role of leadership in today's emphasis on transformation, consciousness, and heart-centered decision-making will resonate with anyone looking to create sustainable change—not only within organizations but within the broader societal framework."

—Dr. Kenneth R. Pelletier
clinical professor of medicine at UCSF, director of the Corporate Health Improvement Program

"*SHIFTS*, isn't just another book on how to lead—it's a blueprint for real, measurable transformation. *SHIFTS* will challenge you to elevate not only your leadership but also your mindset. It's a guide for anyone serious about making an impact."

—Dr. Bradley Nelson
author of *The Emotion Code*, and founder of Discover Healing

"This book is a remarkable road map for anyone looking to elevate their leadership skills and mindset. In a world increasingly shaped by technology and rapid change, *SHIFTS* encourages us to foster a culture of empathy and understanding, which is essential for success. Read this book if you are striving to lead with purpose and create lasting positive impact."

—Alex Bäcker, PhD
innovator, multiple patent holder, author of *101 Clues to a Happy Life*

"This book serves as a powerful blueprint for fostering authentic connections and driving meaningful impact within teams. A must-read for anyone ready to unlock their leadership potential."

—Adam Markel
CEO of More Love Media, author of *Change Proof*

"What a remarkable playbook for leaders who want to cultivate a winning mindset and inspire greatness in others!"

—Jay Paterno
author of *BLITZED!*

"*SHIFTS* is a transformative guide for leaders ready to embrace a more dynamic and visually engaging approach to leadership. Adeyemi's emphasis on seeing and hearing goes beyond the surface, encouraging leaders to draw out insights and foster genuine connections with their teams."

—Tamás Járdán
leadership and high-performance coach,
founder of *Coaching by Drawing*™ method

"This book masterfully guides leaders through the kind of mindset transformation that truly sparks lasting change. For anyone serious about leading with purpose and building a legacy of success, *SHIFTS* is the road map you've been waiting for!"

—Hilary DeCesare
CEO of The Relaunch Co., author of
RELAUNCH! Spark Your Heart to Ignite Your Life

"This is a refreshing take on leadership, blending practical strategies with mindful self-awareness. Dr. Adeyemi shows that true leadership begins with mastering your mindset—developing the ability to see clearly, listen deeply, and act with intention."

—Julie Potiker
mindfulness expert, author of *SNAP! From Chaos to Calm*

"What a powerful guide for leaders looking to evolve their leadership skills and mindsets. His focus on bridging cultural and generational gaps is especially timely, offering leaders a clear path to navigate today's complex world."

—Kimberly Faith
systems thinking expert, author of *Your Lion Inside*

"Dr. Sam Adeyemi's *SHIFTS* is a remarkable guide for conscious leadership and personal transformation. He brilliantly weaves together the elements of vision, intuition, and strategic action to help leaders create positive, lasting change."

—Marie Diamond
globally recognized feng shui master, award-winning speaker inducted to the Speakers Hall of Fame, bestselling author of *Your Home Is a Vision Board*

"I resonated deeply with the concept of the human mind being like a camera, absorbing all that its sees and hears. He describes that by feeding the mind the right inputs, you can powerfully shift your mindset and leverage it to manifest your vision for success. *SHIFTS* is one of those powerful inputs for the camera of your mind."

—Vish Chatterji, MBA
executive coach, founder of Head & Heart Insights, author of *The Business Casual Yogi*; and *Astrology Decoded*

"As we navigate the complexities of leadership, this book serves as a powerful reminder that true transformation begins within, allowing us to create environments that celebrate diversity and foster connection."

—Apela Colorado, PhD
author of *Woman Between the Worlds:* founder and president, Worldwide Indigenous Science Network

"Dr. Adeyemi empowers leaders to master their mindset and lead with vision, purpose, and insight. This book is a must-read for anyone looking to guide their team or organization toward lasting, positive change."

—Dr. Alan Lindemann
obstetrician, maternal health expert, author of *Pregnancy Your Way: Choose a Safe and Happy Birth*

"Dr. Sam Adeyemi has crafted a powerful guide to leadership with *SHIFTS*. His ability to break down the complex journey of leading into clear, actionable steps makes this book an invaluable resource. This book will inspire leaders at every level to create meaningful, lasting impact."

—Ken Foster
author of *The Courage to Change Everything*,
podcast host of *Voices of Courage*

"With 45,000 graduated students and over three million CEOs as friends, I focused on every word Dr. Sam Adeyemi said!"

—Tony DUrso
host of *The Tony DUrso Show*, author of
Imen of Atlantis: Bitten

SHIFTS

6 STEPS TO TRANSFORM YOUR MINDSET AND ELEVATE YOUR LEADERSHIP

SAM ADEYEMI

WILEY

Published by John Wiley & Sons, Inc., Hoboken, New Jersey.
Published simultaneously in Canada.

For general information on our other products and services or for technical support, please contact our Customer Care Department within the United States at (800) 762-2974, outside the United States at (317) 572-3993 or fax (317) 572-4002.

Wiley also publishes its books in a variety of electronic formats. Some content that appears in print may not be available in electronic formats. For more information about Wiley products, visit our web site at www.wiley.com.

Library of Congress Cataloging-in-Publication Data is Available:

ISBN 9781394277728 (Cloth)
ISBN 9781394277773 (ePDF)
ISBN 9781394277759 (epub)

Cover Design: Wiley
Author Photo: Courtesy of the Author

SKY10093737_121924

To all alumni of the Daystar Leadership Academy: Thank you for making small and big SHIFTS wherever you are, transforming our world.

Contents

Introduction

Welcome to SHIFTS

It was a sunny afternoon. Our youth event was to start at 2 p.m. To my surprise, heavy rain descended at about half-past one o'clock. I panicked. How would people attend the entertainment event we had spent months preparing? As the leader of our youth group, I was very concerned. It was the first major event for which I had mobilized a large number of young people. We had gone all around our city inviting other young people to the event we'd tagged as *The Youth Carnival*, promising a day of music, comedy, and a lot more. Now, a disaster was looming. Thankfully, the rain's intensity soon spent itself, and it stopped after about 15 minutes. The clouds cleared, and the sun began to shine again. Within minutes, people began to trickle into the hotel venue. Eventually, the room's capacity was maxed out and we had a very successful event.

In conceiving, planning, and executing the event – which was like nothing I'd ever attempted before – I was testing the principles I had learned from reading *The Fourth Dimension* by David Yonggi Cho, founder of the largest single congregation in the world.[1] In my journey through the book, I discovered that our imagination is so powerful that any picture that is sustained in our mind over time will attract or produce its material equivalent. I was very curious to identify the steps for going from dream to reality.

I had read Cho's book as part of my own personal development plan, a transformative journey that would soon accelerate at a simple dinner with my wife, which we'll discuss further in Chapter 1. Seeing the power of a simple vision come to life filled me with awe, and ingrained in me the idea that small, intentional shifts in the way we choose to perceive our lives and the world around us can have exponential effects. I continued to think, read, discuss, and dream all that I was learning, which eventually led me to formalize the life-changing discoveries I'd made into a set of simple principles I could teach others. That process, which I call *SHIFTS*, is what this book is about.

You hold in your hand a set of ideas that can transform your mindset and elevate your leadership. Why am I so confident that you will achieve such an ambitious transformation? Because you would not even be reading this book if you did not already hold in your heart a desire to accomplish bigger and bolder things!

Today we live in a rapidly changing global landscape in which leaders everywhere must elevate their leadership mindset in order to evolve and succeed. This requires flexibility, adaptability, foresight, and dedication. Being a transformative and open-minded leader in the 21st century is not just a role. It is a mindset – one that embraces innovation, collaboration, and growth. These leadership qualities are essential for driving change, inspiring teams, and navigating the ever-changing landscape.

In this book, you will learn about the following:

- Developing self-leadership to gain intrinsic motivations, beneficial habits, and creativity so you can practice what you preach

- Being mindful of and working toward eliminating age and culture gaps, which can negatively affect the productivity and morale of any team
- Leading from around the corner or around the world by making your presence felt, hiring for talent, and working transparency into the process

On the following pages, I provide you with a step-by-step blueprint to become a transformational leader who inspires and motivates others, and gets the best out of yourself. You will learn about your conscious and subconscious mind's ability to access your thoughts and ideas to create a great variety of positive mind shifts. The mind shifts are represented in each chapter using the common thread from the Six Steps to Transform Your Mindset and Elevate Your Leadership model:

- **See:** You are the sum of what you repeatedly See.
- **Hear:** You are the sum of what you repeatedly Hear.
- **Insight:** Your insights and feelings anchor your beliefs about yourself and the world.
- **Formulate:** Your belief system Formulates your decisions and creates habits.
- **Transform:** Your decisions Transform your actions for making those big, bold moves!
- **Succeed:** Your actions lead to Success.

SHIFTS is an easy-to-remember acronym that will help you increase the impact of your leadership as you apply the steps at personal, organizational, national, and global levels. This is a repeatable and proven process for transforming your life.

All of these steps together equal success. Each step is a building block that ultimately determines who you become as a leader. As you work toward becoming a transformational leader, you can guide others through the process alongside you. This is leadership.

What's to Come

In each chapter, I break down the Six Steps of Transformational Leadership into detail:

- In Chapter 1 I define what each step of the SHIFTS acronym is and the power collective steps can offer to you and your transformative leadership.

- Chapter 2 covers the concept that transformative leadership begins with self-leadership, specifically by taking control of what you allow yourself to See and Hear. This chapter will guide you through the first steps of applying the six-step model on a personal level.

- Chapter 3 focuses on the concepts of acquiring Insight and Formulating new ideas and innovative approaches, including the first steps for applying six steps to your teams.

- Chapter 4 wraps up the acronym by discussing the power this model gives us to Transform our lives and organizations before moving on to discuss the importance of ongoing commitment to future Success.

- Chapter 5 returns to an individual level to further explore the ways we can facilitate deep, lasting personal SHIFTS, specifically with regard to the values we select, embrace, and champion to others. It then discusses the ways that an organization's value system stems from the values of the individuals who comprise it, and it hones in on the importance of intentionally cultivating your culture's values, rather than letting them develop by accident.

- Chapter 6 returns to a wider view, focusing on developing a leadership style that works in multigenerational teams who, in the world of remote work, are often working across large physical distances in addition to the generational gaps that exist in the modern workplace.

- Chapter 7 takes an even larger view, zooming out to look at the SHIFTS that are possible at the national and even global levels. The world is large, but it has become a much smaller place now that distances are closed by technology. As a global leader, you need cultural agility and humility to relate across cultures.

- The Conclusion summarizes the SHIFTS approach, pointing readers to examples of successful SHIFTS from my own life and the lives of others and encouraging them to continue to iterate the SHIFTS process over and over, always moving their life toward the one they've dreamed for themselves.

Each chapter includes useful exercises, stumbling blocks to watch out for, and a summary of key takeaways you can refer back to later. By the time you finish reading this book, you will truly see the power you can have in your own life, and in the lives of others. Transforming your mind set and elevating your leadership ultimately boil down to the fact that you are in control of making the changes you wish to see in the world, starting with yourself.

Achieving a SHIFTS mindset will take time, commitment, and devotion to build a better, strength-based organization.

I can say without hesitation that I have lived and taught this formula successfully worldwide – from Dubai to Denver, Morocco to Maine. If you're reading this book, I know that you're up for the challenge. Using the SHIFTS process, you'll begin developing leadership at every level, just a little bit faster. Plus, you'll be raising your existing leadership teammates to higher levels of performance and productivity. In today's world, the term *leader* has more influence and relevance than ever, especially in a multicultural, multigenerational workplace. Yes, sometimes we are called on to do more with less. But often we build more and thrive as a result.

The key is to start where you are. If encouragement is needed, give it. If people are confused, communicate with them. When you see employees disengaged, engage them. It's my desire that the SHIFTS model will be your step-by-step field guide to a more enthusiastic, creative, and agile workplace. Are you with me?

It is my vision for this book to inspire the next genera-tion of transformative leaders who are not just ready but are excited to embark on a journey of personal discovery toward endless possibility. Leaders like you can light the way for-ward by being beacons of optimism, hope, values, and inspi-ration. Your achievements today pave the way for tomorrow, a path built on bold and innovative ideas, steadfast optimism, and a resolute commitment to building a world in which all people of all nations can thrive. Say goodbye right now to scarcity thinking. With this book, the best is yet to come. I am by your side.

–Sam Adeyemi

SHIFTS

Don't just rewrite a new story,
live it out!

SEE	You are the sum of what you repeatedly See.
HEAR	You are the sum of what you repeatedly Hear.
INSIGHT	Your Insight and feelings anchor your beliefs about yourself and the world.
FORMULATE	Your belief system Formulates your decisions and creates habits.
TRANSFORM	Your decisions Transform your actions for making those big, bold moves!
SUCCEED	Your actions lead to Success. No, you're not dreaming!

Chapter 1

The Power of SHIFTS

The Power of Mindset Shifts

Life has only one certainty: Things are going to change. In a world that shifts constantly beneath your feet, the ability to shift your mindset and adapt might be the most powerful tool you possess. This book is about more than just changing how you think – it's about transforming your entire approach to life, leadership, and success. By making shifts in both your conscious and subconscious mind, you can unlock new possibilities and experience profound change, empowering yourself to lead a life of purpose and guide others toward positive transformation.

Leadership demands more than just strategic vision; it requires the ability to embrace and create change within individuals and organizations. The leverage that comes from shifting mindsets is unmatched, enabling leaders to catalyze meaningful progress in their teams, companies, and communities. This pivotal moment, full of unprecedented challenges and opportunities, is the ideal time for experiencing and leading positive shifts that can reshape our families, organizations, and nations.

Prepare yourself for a journey of transformation, where each chapter will guide you through practical steps to achieve these powerful shifts. The strategies and insights shared in this book are not theoretical; they are grounded in real-world experiences and extensive research. Join me on this journey, where you will transform your own mindset and develop the tools to lead others in making life-changing shifts that propel them toward their greatest potential.

If you can create shifts in your mind, not just your conscious mind but also your subconscious mind and heart, you will experience seismic shifts in real life. Then, if you can inspire others to join you in shifting their outlook, you will enable them to create lasting, positive change in their lives, individually and collectively. Shifting mindsets gives leaders leverage. More than ever, this is a time for us to experience positive shifts in our families, organizations, and nations.

Get ready to feel the SHIFTS. I'm not talking about changing the brand products you buy, or taking dance lessons, or waking up each day an hour earlier. I'm speaking about big SHIFTS – the kind you feel when tectonic plates realign and the earth itself moves under your feet. It is my desire that you feel this same sort of energy as you read this book. It is my desire that you will experience SHIFTS as you learn to apply and practice the lessons I provide within these pages. I call them the Six Steps to Transformation. Think of these steps as simple guideposts to direct you and help you to more clearly understand the power of my SHIFTS process model.

SHIFTS is a practical, yet powerful, acronym that includes the following parts: **See, Hear, Insight, Formulate, Transform, and Succeed**.

In Chapters 2–5, we will delve deeper into this transformative model and learn how to apply each step effectively. But before we dive in, I'd like to share my commitment to this process and what qualifies me to write this book.

This is a book based on evidence, including surveys I've initiated worldwide using qualitative and quantitative results, and by practicing the principles of SHIFTS every day. I built a thriving and profitable leadership organization using these very principles, despite beginning with limited funds and resources. I did this by methodically shifting, one step at a time, elevating my leadership abilities from the ground up. Simply put, think of this process as building blocks – one on top of the other. You add one block at a time, elevating each subsequent block higher and higher. The SHIFTS method uses the same concept: common sense and skill development, applying competency after competency, all resulting in a level of leadership and confidence you perhaps didn't imagine possible.

My beginnings were extremely humble. But here's a solid first lesson – humility is a good thing. It's often part of a recipe for ongoing success. Humility keeps your actions in balance and checks your ego at the door. However, none of what I endured really matters now. You start where you are. We all start where we are. No matter your starting line, your history does not have to predict your future; by making critical SHIFTS, you can envision and begin living a new tomorrow. This is called *visioning*, which is part of SHIFTS (the See and Hear principles), and there are many ways to envision new possibilities. Later in this chapter, we'll see some examples.

First, let's look at today. Today I own and operate numerous businesses, employ hundreds of people, have proudly graduated more than 52,000 individuals from the Daystar Leadership Academy I started, and minister to over 40,000 people onsite and online weekly at the church we founded. I've had the privilege to consult and coach with world leaders, accrue millions of social media followers, earn a respected place in high-profile publications like *FORBES* and others as a regular contributor and columnist, appear on well-known podcasts, and I am honored to be a sought-after keynote speaker at international conferences.

Here is something I want you to know and relate to with confidence. You and I are very similar, even though we each have our own unique story. It is this commonality of the human spirit and love as a business strategy that binds us together, rather than pulls us apart.

How did I accomplish all that? Let's start by taking our first look at SHIFTS.

Introduction to SHIFTS: Six Steps to Transformation

In the rapidly evolving landscape of leadership, the ability to adapt and inspire change has never been more crucial. At the heart of this adaptability lies the power of SHIFTS – a transformative model designed to elevate leaders by reshaping their mindset and tactics. SHIFTS is more than just an acronym; it is a guiding framework that leads to profound personal and organizational transformation.

As mentioned, **SHIFTS** stands for **See, Hear, Insight, Formulate, Transform, Succeed** – each step representing a critical phase in the journey of leadership development:

See: The first step involves cultivating the vision to recognize opportunities and challenges in your environment. Great leaders must be able to see beyond the obvious, identifying patterns and potential that others might miss.

Hear: Listening is the foundation of understanding. Effective leaders must not only listen to what is being said but also develop the ability to catch what remains unsaid – the underlying concerns, motivations, and aspirations of their teams and stakeholders.

Insight: Insight comes from synthesizing what you've seen and heard. It's about connecting distant dots, understanding unspoken implications, and gaining a clear perspective that informs decision-making.

Formulate: Armed with insight, the next step is to formulate strategies and plans that are both innovative and practical. This stage requires creativity, critical thinking, and the ability to translate vision into actionable steps.

Transform: Transformation is where vision meets action. This step involves implementing the strategies, driving change, and ensuring that the shift from plan to practice is smooth and effective.

Succeed: The final step is achieving success – not just in terms of outcomes but also in fostering a culture of continuous improvement and adaptability. Success here is measured by the ability to sustain positive change and inspire ongoing growth.

The SHIFTS model is not just a basic checklist or a series of steps; it is a mindset – a way of approaching leadership that integrates vision, understanding, and action. By internalizing these principles, leaders can make the necessary mental shifts that lead to tangible success. Each component of SHIFTS builds on the last, creating a comprehensive approach to leadership that is dynamic, responsive, and forward-thinking.

In leadership, success is often determined by the ability to adapt and evolve in response to new challenges. The SHIFTS model provides a structured framework without sacrificing the flexibility that enables leaders to navigate change effectively. By adopting this mindset, you are not only preparing yourself to lead through transformation but also empowering those around you to achieve their fullest potential.

Leadership success is rooted in the ability to inspire and enact change. SHIFTS equips you with the tools and mindset necessary to do just that – leading with clarity, insight, and purpose. As you progress through this book, you will learn how to apply each step of the SHIFTS model, transforming not only your leadership style but also the impact you have on those you lead. Embrace these shifts and watch as they propel you and your organization toward unprecedented success.

 The Window Table

One evening, many years ago, I took my beautiful wife, Nike, out to dinner at a restaurant near our home in Lagos, Nigeria. It wasn't a high-class restaurant. Our income wasn't much at that time, so we went for what was affordable. It was dark outside, and you could see the headlights of cars moving up and down the street. The restaurant was located on a high street, and we could see different colors of light from billboards. Suddenly, I saw an opportunity and grabbed it. It was an opportunity to sell Nike a vision.

We were seated at a table by a window. I told her to look outside. Then I asked her to close her eyes and to forget we were in Lagos. I told her to imagine that we were in New York or some other famous city. There and then, I made her a promise that I would take her all over the world and we would eat at nice restaurants. To this day, each time we visit a new city and happen to eat in a restaurant, I remember that night in Lagos. The vision has become our reality. We became the people in the vision. We shifted our minds first, and then the SHIFTS happened in our lives later.

Everything you'll read in this book stems from that one simple moment of clarity, when Nike and I realized that we could close our eyes to the circumstances around us, envision the world we wanted to inhabit, and begin the process of incremental change that becomes its own feedback loop, leading inevitably to the life you've envisioned.

I know that you have a vision for your life, and I know that you can become the leader you've always dreamed of being. Those visions can become very powerful, as we'll see in some of the remarkable stories I'll share throughout later chapters. And you and I both have the drive to succeed, but first we have to tap into our inner being. Yes, there will be challenges along the way and stumbling blocks. I had many of them in my youth growing up in Africa. All of my original plans fell apart early in life, but I learned how to SHIFT my thinking, and I'm sharing it all here in this book so that you can do it, too.

As I said previously, it doesn't matter where you're starting from. Nike and I began our SHIFT at a simple window side table in Lagos, Nigeria. Likewise, your location will not determine your success. Only you determine how high you can soar and what you can overcome. I believe that the stories I share in this book can help you to shift your thinking and literally transform your life. I'll be with you every step of the way, guiding you through the practical, real-world techniques and tools in this book.

In this book, I will not only be sharing my own personal stories of inner growth and extraordinary transformation but I'll also be sharing firsthand real-world stories from those I've coached or mentored using this life-changing process. I've included my own leadership growth, which highlights the trials and tribulations of being a global business leader. So get ready to shift from a "Why me?" mentality to "Why not me?" consciousness. This book will help you to stop asking,

"Why do things never work out for me?" I understand. There was a time when I felt that certain blessings would never be mine, and although I lived with gratitude for what I did have, I desired more for my life.

Out of College and My Future Came to a Dead Halt

I was fresh out of college when I experienced one of the most depressing episodes of my life. I graduated as a civil engineer, and the plan had always been that I would work at my father's construction company. I suppose the lesson here is that not all your plans work out as you think they will. Sometimes there's a larger plan, one with bigger ideas for you than you dreamed for yourself. Well, on graduation, my plan evaporated into thin air as my father's business closed. Just like that – no job! That incident dealt such an emotional blow to my soul, and I was flooded with such despair. I felt trapped and stuck! I was jobless for two years, certain my future – out of my control – had gone from bright to gloomy in an instant.

But eventually, instead of beating the drum of discontent about how terrible the situation was, I decided to put my energy and resources into reading and learning, just like you're doing now. I stayed open to the idea that there was a path forward to a better future, and I determined that I would discover it and investigate it. But once I knew what it was, what principles would I need to apply? I wasn't sure, but I knew there must be something. In other words, I was searching for the formula to a better life. The exciting thing is that the SHIFTS Six Steps to Transformation process in this book can be adapted into a perfect formula for your life, too.

The only instruction that I am offering is that you implement these action steps: adapt, delete, modify, and expand to suit your specific needs. No one walks in your shoes but you. If you come across information that you can adapt to your specific leadership journey, then do so. If you find material that is not relatable to your business, then ignore it. If you find information in this book that can be tweaked and modified to fit your business structure, your leadership style, or your long-term plans for success, then by all means, go right ahead. And most important, feel free to expand on any ideas you find here. That's where the nuggets of gold can be found. Your participation in this book is what will make it memorable and long-lasting. You're the one who will make the contents of this book even better. So I thank you in advance.

Successful Leaders Are Also Readers

I began to read voraciously, and there were three books that changed my life's trajectory. Though they were different books, they shared similar themes – principles that had to do with my attitude and beliefs. Attitude can be everything. How we manage and control our life creates the very foundation of what we aim for and how we execute our dreams. I'll even take it so far as to say that your attitude can control your ultimate destiny, help you achieve mastery, and help you reach your goals easier and faster.

> How we think shows through in how we act. Attitudes are mirrors of the mind. They reflect our thinking.
> —David Joseph Schwartz

Surprised? This all surprised me too, because until this point, I had believed that success was fact-based and built on the pillars of "do more, get more." I was wrong. I learned that the results I truly desired required an attitude change so absolute that it would shift my heart's core. I also realized that if I could shift my mind and think differently, my heart would follow, and my results would reflect that. This is a key point. When thoughts move from our conscious mind to our subconscious mind, we create habits. Positive habits create positive actions, which lead to better results. Wise leaders know the importance of positive habits, yet applying this wisdom to one's life can feel like an uphill climb. It might be the reason more people don't feel joy in their careers and lives. If it were easy, everyone would do it, right?

The books that influenced me most and caused major shifts to my mind, heart, and habits were *Tough Times Never Last but Tough People Do!* by Robert H. Schuller, *Think and Grow Rich* by Napoleon Hill and Rosa Lee Beeland, and *As a Man Thinketh* by British philosopher James Allen. In his work, Robert Schuller pointed out that "Attitudes are more important than facts," a quote attributed to George MacDonald. That was a brain-shifter for me. Are facts not sacred? What could be more important than facts?

Schuller's words shifted my focus away from what was not working on my outside, forcing me to address what was not working on my inside. Then the title of Napoleon Hill's book began to shift my mind, even before I read the content. *Think and grow rich*! I had always believed that what you needed to do to make money was to work hard. Hill's emphasis on thinking *first* got my attention and made me buy the book immediately. In Allen's book I found the line

"You cannot travel within and stand still without."[1] His point hit me like a lightning bolt. If I could experience big shifts on my inside, it was inevitable that corresponding big shifts would happen on my outside. As leaders we cannot stand outside of ourselves and attempt to peer inside. Our awareness and strength grow from the inside out. This became a major paradigm shift in my thinking, and it has reaped benefits in business and in all areas of my life ever since, in both good times and hard times.

The Heart of the Matter Is a Matter of the Heart

Rick Warren, best-selling author of *The Purpose Driven Life: What on Earth Am I Here For?*, says, "The heart of the matter is a matter of the heart."[2] I desperately wanted to become someone worthy of all I dreamed – the person I knew I truly was inside of me. And do you know what? I found that person, and you can, too. This became a model for creating massive shifts in my heart. I believe these steps are revolutionary and life altering, and once you grasp them, they will create nonstop transformation in your life, too. By the way, I created an easy-to-use, simple-to-follow process model that is also featured in the back of this book for your fast reference and application.

To lead with conviction, I suggest diving within yourself first. Going deep. When we peek under the hood of our own habits and beliefs, we gain insights we didn't understand before. Perhaps this is why we often find ourselves in places we'd rather not look. Les Brown said, "For you to do something you have never done before, you need to become someone you have never been before."

My promise to you is that this book will enable you to root into who you want to be. It will also give you the capacity to guide others toward their own transformation, and isn't that the essence of a true leader? It's having the ability to bring out the very best in everyone around you, regardless of title, status, income, or past mistakes. A person's past is never an accurate predictor of their future; what they have been before can truly become something new, enabling them to create the life they yearn to create and live out loud.

Before moving on, take a moment to sit back and consider all you've read so far. Just like Nike and me dreaming at our restaurant window, close your eyes and picture the world you'd create for yourself, if you could jettison all the negative thoughts, habits, and baggage that have held you down so far. Let yourself think big and dream loud for a moment; when you're done, come back and read on to begin moving forward and upward. See Figure 1.1 for a visual of the SHIFTS Process Model.

The SHIFTS model sets the creative tone and road map for this entire book and your personal experience. This can easily become a repeatable and proven process at all levels: individual, organizational, national, and global.

Lessons are often easier to apply when they are broken down into easy steps. The SHIFTS Six Steps to Transformation will shift your life if you let it guide you. In the back of this book, you will see again a graphic depiction of this acronym so that you can reference it quickly and efficiently. Tear it out, make a copy, or snap a pic with your phone so it's always at hand, ready to be used on the go. Refer to the steps as you need them. Put it up where you will see it often. SHIFTS is a

Figure 1.1 SHIFTS Process Model

reliable navigational tool when used in tandem with your leadership journey. I created this so that at a glance you'll be able to see the bigger picture of what it takes to be the architect of your own success story.

Research shows us that when we see the bigger picture and envision what we want to achieve, we can navigate our way there. When we do this, our chances for success increase exponentially, and our life itself SHIFTS. Take time to learn about the Six Steps to Transform Your Mindset and Elevate Your Leadership.

Sources Gathered for This Book

The research compiled for this book consists of interviews with hundreds of CEOs and executives worldwide, including training professionals and business leaders. This book's content is evidence-based from a specific professional survey my organization conducted over a period of several months on a global scale, along with other findings. The results are a critical part of this leadership book. I asked for and gathered your input, insights, suggestions, and queries. We then broke down the quantitative and qualitative data assigned to various regions around the world. Somewhere, you are in this book. If any of these statements describe you, I believe you might be ready for SHIFTS in your life that elevate your leadership mindset. Do you fit one of these descriptions?

- A leader whose career could use a reboot
- An aspiring entrepreneur
- A business owner ready for change or expansion

- A training or coaching professional in need of new ideas
- An eager, ready-to-get-started emerging leader
- A virtual provider of leadership techniques and tools
- Someone ready to reinvent themselves and help others

No one is born with a leadership gene. Leaders are nurtured and developed. Anyone can lead when they are provided with empathy, resources, and updated information. I'm asking you to trust the process, and the process will reciprocate.

As human beings and leaders, it is our tendency to search for happiness, success, personal and professional satisfaction, and a flourishing life for our children, family, and friends. Grueling courses on these subjects – once called *soft* – are now taught at prestigious universities like Yale, Stanford, and the London School of Business. A great example is the popular undergraduate course offered at Yale University, called *Life Worth Living: A Guide to What Matters Most*. Taught by the book's authors (Volf, Croasmun, and McAnnally-Linz), this program has become a worldwide phenomenon.[3] I, too, am proud to say that this book you're holding offers its own coursework with Six Steps to Transformation – transformation that is undeniably transcendent, joy-filled, and tool-oriented for tweaking the ups, downs, ins, and outs of a more fulfilling and satisfying life and leadership journey. Think of it as a crash course in finding your way to what matters most. The following are self-discovery exercises for SHIFTS in visioning.

Exercise Visualizing Your Current Mindsets and Desired Shifts

Objective: To help you identify your current mindsets and visualize the shifts you need to make in order to achieve your leadership goals.

INSTRUCTIONS

Find a Quiet Space: Begin by finding a quiet, comfortable space where you can focus without distractions. It helps to have a notepad or sketchbook handy to jot down notes or images for future reference.

Visualization Preparation: Close your eyes and take a few deep breaths to center yourself. Think about your current role as a leader. Consider your daily routines, decision-making processes, interactions with your team, and the challenges you face.

Visualize Your Current Mindset: Imagine a typical day in your leadership role. Visualize how you approach your tasks, how you respond to challenges, and how you interact with others.

Reflect on your emotions during these moments. Do you feel confident, stressed, uncertain, or inspired? Identify the underlying beliefs or attitudes that guide your behavior and decisions, and sketch or note them before moving on.

Visualize Your Desired Shift: Now, envision what your ideal leadership approach would look like. How would you like to respond to challenges? What kind of leader do you aspire to be?

Picture yourself embodying these qualities. Imagine leading with clarity, confidence, empathy, and decisiveness. Visualize the positive impact this shift has on your team, your organization, and your own sense of fulfillment. Add these positive notes or images next to the challenges and frustrations you noted before.

Compare and Contrast: After you have a clear picture of both your current and desired mindsets, compare them. What are the key differences between where you are now and where you want to be?

Identify the specific shifts you need to make in your thinking, behavior, or approach to bridge the gap between your current and desired leadership mindset, and draw or note them as the bridge between the negative images you started with and the positive places you intend to land.

Action Plan: Write down three specific actions you can take in the next week to start making these shifts. These could be small adjustments in how you approach a particular challenge, changes in your communication style, or new practices you want to integrate into your leadership routine.

Exercise Journaling for Self-Reflection on Leadership Challenges

EXERCISE 1

Objective: This exercise will guide you through a series of journaling prompts to help you reflect on your personal leadership challenges and explore how making mindset shifts can address these challenges.

INSTRUCTIONS

Set Aside Time: Choose a time when you can write without interruptions, allowing yourself to fully engage in the reflection process.

(continued)

(continued)

Journaling Prompts:

Identifying Challenges: What are the top three challenges you face as a leader right now?

How do these challenges affect your ability to lead effectively?

What emotions do these challenges evoke in you (e.g. frustration, anxiety, motivation)?

Exploring Mindsets: What beliefs or assumptions do you hold that might be contributing to these challenges?

Are there any patterns in your thinking or behavior that you notice when dealing with these challenges?

How do you currently respond to these challenges? Is this response effective, or does it need to shift?

Envisioning Solutions: If you could approach these challenges with a different mindset, what would that look like?

What new perspectives or attitudes would help you overcome these obstacles?

How might changing your mindset positively influence your actions and outcomes?

Commitment to Change: What specific mindset shifts do you need to make to address these challenges?

What is one step you can take today to start making these shifts?

How will you hold yourself accountable for implementing these changes?

Review and Reflect: After completing the journaling prompts, review your responses. Consider how the insights you've gained can be integrated into your daily leadership practice. You might want to physically write them into your daily agenda or add them as reminders to your phone or laptop calendar.

Ongoing Reflection: Set a reminder to revisit these journaling prompts in a few weeks. Reflect on the progress you've made and note any new challenges or shifts that have emerged.

These exercises are designed to help you connect deeply with your current leadership approach and identify actionable steps toward transformation. By engaging in these reflective practices, you'll be better equipped to make the necessary SHIFTS that will elevate your leadership effectiveness.

Group Work (for Organizational Leaders)

Just as you did individually, have your team create a document that envisions a workplace of self-discovery. This will look different for every team; the key is to achieve consensus on what the ideal workplace would look and feel like. The document is a sort of a commandment list of how this particular team wants to be seen and heard. Here's an example one of my teams developed as their workplace of self-discovery and meaning.

Pay attention to and practice these seven steps for SHIFTing behaviors and outcomes on the job:

1. **Leadership behaviors shift.** Stay on top of it. Pay attention. Is our team paying attention to body language and cultural and age-related sensitivities? Humor is fun; making fun of others isn't. Know the difference. Every week someone offers a team building activity first thing in the morning. Everyone shares their expertise and helps others to excel. Discuss written and verbal skills. This affects

company culture. We've noticed that we don't communicate like we used to, and we'd like to recapture that sense of a shared vocabulary. Communication moves rapidly, but it still must make sense and be correct for the team to understand direction and shift forward. Come up with your own signals or abbreviations, team talk, or sensible comments to move things along. Don't send lengthy emails, texts, or engage in endless, meaningless discussions or meetings. Communicate like a journalist: get to the point . . . make the point . . . move on. No matter what your industry, we're all in the communication and relationship business. These are the two things that shift our world and build trust.

2. **Help others defuse stress.** Stress is an inevitable part of the workplace due to a wide variety of reasons, but stress doesn't have to mean frayed tempers. When you notice visible signs of stress, ask people what they think triggers stressful situations, then try to avoid those triggers. Implement patient behavior. Be the example. Don't get too personal but show empathy. If someone needs additional help outside the office, have resources ready to provide. Show you care without being nosy or insensitive. People love it when others care about them.

3. **Mentor expected behavior.** Live and lead the standards you expect from others. Be the person in the mirror.

4. **Challenge people to try new things outside their comfort zone.** This initiates SHIFTS faster than anything. People love to stretch their abilities if it's a safe environment and they won't be made fun of. Laugh together, not at one another. Cheer your teammates on! Use judgment; don't pass judgment.

5. **Build internal coaching teams.** This is the fastest way to a leader's success. Coaching others sends a big message. It says, "I believe in you." "You've got this." Create a fun environment. Welcome all kinds of feedback. Then ask people how they would best receive feedback, especially when it's constructive. Never embarrass someone. That's a no-win. Everyone welcomes better communication tips if there is trust and skill behind it.

6. **Don't play favorites.** Let everyone have a say. Never assume someone is taking care of something. Ask.

   Complacency kills team spirit. Keep raising the bar.

   Don't assume everyone on the team shares your vision. Paint a picture of how your vision can benefit everyone. If it doesn't work for everyone now, explain how it might help in the months ahead. Give people a chance to accept and understand changes. If people resist, don't persist. Take time to make important changes that create comfort and respect.

7. **Give praise in progress.** Don't wait six months to correct a situation. Commit on the spot to helping someone correct and redirect. This will save you and the entire team tons of time shifting forward.

As you engage in the SHIFTS exercises – visualizing your current and desired mindsets and journaling about leadership challenges – you might encounter certain stumbling blocks. These are common barriers that can impede your progress, but by recognizing and addressing them, you can move forward with greater clarity and determination. Here's what to expect and how to overcome these obstacles.

Stumbling Blocks and Strategies to Overcome Them

1. Resistance to Change

Stumbling Block: Resistance to change is one of the most common stumbling blocks leaders face. It can manifest as a reluctance to let go of familiar routines, fear of the unknown, or discomfort with stepping outside of your comfort zone. Even when you know that change is necessary, the inertia of staying the same can be powerful.

How It Ties to the Exercises: In the Visualization Exercise, you might notice that when you visualize your desired leadership mindset, there's a part of you that clings to the old ways of thinking or acting. This resistance can surface as doubt about whether the new mindset will work or whether you're capable of making the change.

Overcoming Resistance:

Acknowledge the Resistance: The first step is to acknowledge that resistance is a natural part of the change process. It's your mind's way of trying to protect you from perceived risks. Recognize it, but don't let it dictate your actions.

Small, Incremental Changes: Break down the shifts into smaller, manageable steps. If a necessary change feels overwhelming, ask yourself, "What's the first small step I can take in this direction?" Then commit to take that step until you're ready for the next one. This approach can make the change feel less daunting and easier to integrate into your daily routine.

Revisit Your Why: Reflect on why these shifts are important. Reconnecting with your deeper motivation – such as the impact you want to have as a leader, or your vision of the life you're determined to build – can help you push through resistance.

2. Overcoming Limiting Beliefs

What to Expect: Limiting beliefs are self-imposed barriers that convince you that you're not capable of achieving your goals or that change isn't possible. These beliefs might include thoughts like "I'm not a natural leader," "I've always done it this way," or "I'm not good enough to succeed."

How It Ties to the Exercises: During the Journaling Exercise, as you reflect on your leadership challenges, you might uncover limiting beliefs that have been holding you back. These beliefs can make it difficult to envision a new way of leading or to believe that the shifts you desire are achievable.

Overcoming Limiting Beliefs:

Identify and Challenge Beliefs: Start by identifying specific limiting beliefs that arise. Ask yourself where these beliefs come from and explore whether they are based on facts or assumptions.

Reframe Your Thinking: Replace limiting beliefs with empowering ones. For example, instead of "I'm not a natural leader," try "I am capable of learning and growing into the leader I'm determined to be."

Focus on Past Successes: Reflect on times when you successfully overcame challenges or made positive changes in your life. Use these experiences as evidence that you can also over-come current limiting beliefs.

3. Fear of Failure

What to Expect: Fear of failure can be a paralyzing stumbling block, preventing you from taking risks or trying new approaches. It's the fear that if you attempt to make these shifts, you might fail, leading to negative consequences or judgment from others.

How It Ties to the Exercises: While engaging in the Visualization Exercise, you might find that fear of fail-ure clouds your vision of success. This fear can keep you anchored in your current mindset, making it dif-ficult to embrace the shifts you need to make.

Overcoming Fear of Failure:

Embrace a Growth Mindset: View failure as a learn-ing opportunity rather than a reflection of your worth. Every attempt, whether successful or not, brings you closer to your goals.

Set Realistic Expectations: Understand that shifts and changes take time. Set realistic expectations for yourself, and take the time to celebrate small victories along the way.

Seek Support: Don't be afraid to seek support from mentors, colleagues, or peers who can offer guid-ance and encouragement as you navigate through these shifts. Ask a trusted coworker or admired friend to have coffee, and be intentional in asking them about their journey and the struggles they've worked through in their journey.

4. Impatience with the Process

What to Expect: Transformation doesn't happen overnight. Impatience can lead to frustration if you don't see immediate results, causing you to abandon the process before the SHIFTS have had a chance to take root.

How It Ties to the Exercises: As you work through the Journaling Exercise, you might feel eager for quick fixes to your leadership challenges. This impatience can make you overlook the importance of gradual, consistent effort.

Overcoming Impatience:

Trust the Process: Understand that the SHIFTS model is a journey, not a sprint. Real change takes time and persistence.

Reflect on Progress: Periodically review your journal entries to see how far you've come. Recognizing small but significant progress can help keep impatience at bay.

Stay Committed: Remind yourself that each small shift contributes to a larger transformation. Stay committed to the process, even when progress seems slow.

By being aware of these stumbling blocks and using the SHIFTS exercises to work through them, you can maintain momentum and continue progressing toward your leadership goals. Remember, the journey of transformation is as important as the destination, and each step you take – no matter how small – brings you closer to becoming the leader you aspire to be.

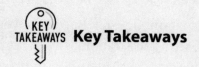

Key Takeaways

In this chapter, we've explored the importance of making SHIFTS to elevate our leadership and personal growth. Goal setting alone is not enough to propel us to the next level. To achieve meaningful progress, we must break down our big ideas into manageable, actionable steps – this is where true transformation occurs. The SHIFTS model offers a structured approach to create change, providing clarity on who our stakeholders are, what milestones we can set, and how to measure success efficiently.

As leaders, we must continuously invite inspiration into our lives, and this chapter has laid the groundwork for that process. We've seen that by chunking down goals, identifying stakeholders, and setting clear milestones, we can build strength under each phase of the SHIFTS transformation model. Success isn't just about reaching the end goal – it's about creating a path that enables us to track and measure our progress along the way.

Now, as we prepare for Chapter 2, we will dive deeper into my personal SHIFTS for building morale, fostering self-development, and increasing self-esteem. Remember, you can't wait for inspiration to strike – you must invite it in. Get ready to start making big, personal SHIFTS as we continue this transformative journey.

Chapter 2

See and Hear

Mastering Leadership Through What You See and Hear

In the journey of transformative leadership, the first SHIFT steps begin with what you See and Hear. These foundational principles of the SHIFTS model emphasize the profound impact that our sensory inputs have on our subconscious mind and, ultimately, on our actions and outcomes as leaders.

Seeing is the process of intentionally curating of the images and visuals that we allow into our minds. The things we consistently expose ourselves to – whether positive or negative – embed deeply within our subconscious, shaping our thoughts, beliefs, and behaviors. This principle teaches us that by deliberately choosing what we see, we can influence our mindset and, by extension, our reality. For example, successful leaders often use tools like vision boards to keep their goals and aspirations in constant view, reinforcing their commitment and driving them toward achievement.

Hearing is often understood as a passive process; however, when I discuss hearing in the context of the SHIFTS process, I mean the act of consciously choosing to carefully focus on the auditory elements that surround us, emphasizing the power of repeated messages. What we allow ourselves to hear regularly – whether it's encouragement, criticism, or even self-talk – conditions our minds to believe and act on those messages. This principle underscores the importance of surrounding ourselves with positive, affirming voices that align with our goals and values.

Together, these principles of See and Hear lay the groundwork for the transformative journey of SHIFTS. By being intentional about what we see and hear, we can begin to reshape our internal landscape, leading to more intentional and effective leadership. As you explore the SHIFTS model, remember that transformation begins with what you allow into your mind – because what you consistently see and hear will ultimately guide your path to success.

When it comes to seeing, vision boards are creative tools that pop the lid off your imagination. It's been called "brainwashing yourself to success." *Brainwashing* is a word that typically has a negative context, but that's only because we think of brainwashing as something forced on us from an external locus of control. When we begin to think of ourselves as the actor, rather than the recipient, of brainwashing, the negative connotations fall away. After all, what does *wash* even mean? To make something clean! To remove the grime and dirt, leaving behind a clean slate! Vision boards give us this power: the ability to strip away the negative imagery that prevents us from having the situation we want and replace it with a picture of the life we're determined to create.

Vison boarding can be as simple as you'd like it to be. If you're a tactile thinker, you might prefer sifting through a magazine or stack of printed images, selecting those that capture your desires, and physically attaching them to a poster or wall in your line of sight. The more tech-oriented among us might prefer to do the same digitally, using any of the online tools or apps at our disposal. Either way, the process of curating a collection of images that represent your goals adds depth and breadth to the overall experience. There are even audio programs that enable you to curate soundscapes that are compatible with your vision to truly maximize the sensory experience!

It might sound basic, but I'll tell you – there is something so nice about giving yourself permission to be a bit childlike and make a simple wish list. After about five years of age, we are often discouraged from a lot of creative thinking. We're even told not to color outside the lines. Can you imagine Steve Jobs or Amelia Earhart, Kobe Bryant or Sally Ride being told this? These are people who understood well that growing up doesn't have to mean growing out of the ability to dream.

This process of vision boarding definitely takes you outside of the boundaries of your own imagination. It became one of the biggest personal SHIFTS in my life. And you can make these SHIFTS, too. My experience happened because I discovered a significant principle: Whatever you see and hear consistently over time will enter your heart (or subconscious mind) and put your life on autopilot! See and Hear are the first two steps of the SHIFTS Transformation Model.

 Step 1: See – You are the sum of what you repeatedly see. What you see day in and day out takes root deep within and will inevitably influence your thoughts and your subconscious mind. Margarida Alpuim and Katja Ehrenberg stated in *Psychology in Journalism* that images have a powerful effect on the mind because they are immediate, circumventing logical analysis to be processed by the brain in the blink of an eye. They also said that images can

See and Hear

affect our emotions more powerfully than words. They are more likely to be remembered by people than information presented in texts, and even add to the perceived "truthiness" of a statement.[1] Here is the point: The things you see don't leave your mind the same, whether the images are positive or negative. Successful people know this, and they are intentional about what they feed their eyes.

TD Bank, known as America's "Most Convenient Bank," surveyed individuals and small business owners across the United States to learn how they practice visualization and the effect that visualization (or lack thereof) had on their financial success.[2] They found out that those who keep photos and vision boards feel twice as confident that they will achieve their goals than those who don't. They also discovered that 82% of small business owners who used vision boards or some form of visioning from the start reported that they had accomplished more than half of their goals. This means that repeatedly seeing certain pictures creates belief, and beliefs affect performance. What you believe is what you become, and you can influence your belief system by changing what you see repeatedly.

Step 2: Hear – You are the sum of what you repeatedly hear. What you hear continuously affects your feelings and also takes root in your subconscious, developing the ability to influence your future behaviors. For example, if your parents repeated something over and over in your childhood, there's a good chance you will repeat that with your own children. A cyclical chain of events is created that spans generations, all based on the words someone heard as a child. People who have lived through wars talk about the sounds they heard and the enormous impact similar sounds have on them to this very day.

Research has confirmed that when we hear something repeatedly, our minds begin to believe the information is true.[3] When we intentionally listen to some information, it can strengthen our belief in the possibility or its reality. If what you are hearing is your goal, your heart feels and your mind believes that you have accomplished it.

LESSONS

How I Learned to Pre-See My Success

In the early 2000s I attended a seminar with my wife, Nike. The speaker declared to the audience that everyone could benefit from creating a dream board where you display your visions, hopes, dreams, intentions, and specific depictions of even a car or home. The facilitator asked that we all include photos that represent our dream car, new home, or whatever we wanted. I thought this was an interesting assignment, and Nike and I were both excited about doing it. He then asked everyone to bring the photo of their dream home back to the conference the next day and told us that if we couldn't find a photo of what we wanted, we should simply draw it – again, etching in our minds what was possible.

We went home that evening, and in our search we found one particular home that we both loved in a Toyota Camry brochure. We cut it out and chuckled because we realized that we'd found our dream home in the background of an ad designed to sell a car. So, dreaming big, we decided that it would be good to throw the car into our vision as well. It was a two-for-one dream board! I gleefully said that if both images are in the same picture, we would be getting both! That evening we tore it out and brought it to the seminar the next day. After the seminar concluded, we tacked the picture up on the wall of our home, where it would be sure to inhabit our vision constantly. My wife is an architect, so she took it a step further, drawing out a floor plan for our future home. It stayed up on that wall, visible day in and day out, for a few years. We walked by and looked at it every day. It became more than a conscious visualization; it began to live in our subconscious goals as well. And guess what happened? Eventually, the house became a reality as we saw the image over and over daily, weekly, monthly, each step closer to our move-in day. Funnily enough, the first thing that materialized was the Toyota Camry. Our eyes were set on it every day, and it became our physical reality – because we made it so.

The simple act of staring down our vision each day affected our decisions and habits. Budgeting became simpler, because we were looking at the things we were saving for so constantly that it seeped into each financial decision. Career decisions became simpler; instead of dreading work on a day when we weren't feeling great, we had a clear picture of exactly what we were going to work for. And, because this was a vision we'd crafted together, these weren't just wood and metal objects – the home and Camry represented the life we'd chosen to build together, and we were determined to dream it into reality.

Seeing something you believe in over and over truly manifests in real life. This concept has been a part of quantum physics teaching for a very long time.

The challenge is not manifesting what you want; it's staying on task, remaining devoted to your dream and then visualizing it daily until it becomes real. This takes discipline and patience – two emotional intelligences to teach your leaders.

From a personal perspective, Nike and I enjoyed participating together in an activity that felt intimate and deeply bonding. And here's the bonus. It can put more romance in your life. There is a process called *calling in the one* (which is another topic), but the concept relates to this same feeling. You can capture a photo of a couple hand-in-hand strolling the beach at dusk or other intimate settings. Or maybe it's an image of a stage surrounded by an audience of thousands, and suddenly you're the one taking center stage! Anything can go into a dream and vision board.

As I noted previously, these visions can be created on any of your electronic devices. We preferred the tactile approach. All I know is that this exercise truly works. To this day, I continue to post images in my home and office that inspire me to make major SHIFTS in my personal and professional life. So far, each one has worked out as planned. If you stick with it, I promise this See and Hear exercise will shift your reality and your mindset. It will ultimately shift your behavior and your results, too. Remember that you're the sum of what you repeatedly see. I not only saw the photos, I envisioned us driving the car and living in the house. The car and house moved from our conscious mind to the subconscious, becoming part of our decisions and actions. Now that's a life-changing shift, and you can do it, too.

The See and Hear part of my process model has the power and capacity to form who you are on the inside. Who we become starts from the inside out, not the other way around. We don't become who we want to be when we have what we want to have; we have what we want to have as the *result* of becoming who we want to be. Knowledge will transform and lift you. It makes you aware, sharper, more conscious, and equipped for life's twists, turns, and ultimate SHIFTS.

What We Consume Makes Us Who We Are

What you consume in your news, world events, business and family matters, and friendships contributes to creating who you are. Everything around you is fighting for your attention, which means it's crucial to develop the practice of *intentional* attention. Are you intentional about the information you consume – the things you listen to, speak out loud, or view each day? When you take all of this into consideration, you start to realize that transformative leadership begins with self-leadership and self-mastery. The ability to lead yourself begins with your desire to create shifts in your own mind. Here are the ways we draw to us information and the impact it might have on our behavior and abilities. It often starts with what we read.

Our family was on vacation in Orlando many years ago and we decided to attend the Christian Booksellers Association Convention. I will never forget what was written on a large banner at the conference: *What goes into a mind comes out in a life*. Reading is a significant way successful leaders study subjects that matter to them and absorb various wisdom.

In evidence-based references at the end of this book, you'll see my notations on various studies and books that contribute to this important idea. One study established that exposure to vocabulary through reading helped children achieve higher scores in different intelligence testing.[4] In Chapter 1, I mention how reading a wide variety of books shifted my paradigm from the frustrating attempt to change my life from the inside out.

Books are available in many formats: e-books, audio versions, braille, and others. Regardless of format, a book is always a wise investment. Almost anywhere on earth, you have afford-able access to decades worth of experience on any topic from a subject matter expert, billionaire, or renowned authority. This creates the opportunity for you to allow the inner reality of a successful person or leader to help shape your own inner land-scape. This is often the deep dive of leadership. The potential return on investment is significant.

This is how you start applying yourself to create your vision: by proactively and intentionally curating the ideas you see and hear. If you're not an avid reader, you can start by making a running list of the books, publications, pod-casts, and videos you want to buy, borrow, subscribe to, or use to start transforming your inner self. If budget is an issue, take heart! You live in the greatest moment for afford-able information in the history of the universe. Many formats are free online, and the enormity of information available now via the internet is mind-boggling. Reading this book is a positive step in this direction, and you might want to use the sources I reference as next steps. I've found that often one idea leads to another. A book might reference an inter-esting article, which leads me to a useful blog post, which references a fascinating podcast, which leads me to another helpful book!

This habit soon becomes a powerful process that continues forward for a lifetime. And it doesn't require reading every single page of every single publication. Some books are best absorbed by selecting parts that speak to you at a particular time in life when you need something to help you get through and will help you to acquire the information you desire on the spot. Films have this same impact. Here is another story and lesson I'll share with you.

The Impact of Movies and Films

When she was in high school, our daughter Adora had a short break, and asked if a friend could come home with her for a visit. Of course we were delighted to welcome her. Her friend had traveled all the way from Europe to attend high school in the United States. Nike observed how amazingly fluent our guest's English was and wanted to know if her schools in Croatia taught the English language. Our visitor replied that she did not learn English in school; she had picked it up by watching American movies. That jolted me a bit. Movies shape our minds, whether we realize it or not. The experience did not end there. Adora and her friend asked us to pick up another schoolmate from a different address and drop them off at a local mall to go shopping. This schoolmate was originally from Asia and was attending classes in the United States. Again, Nike observed her smooth, fluent English, including an American accent. We asked if English was taught in her country. The schoolmate replied that it was not taught in her country, and that she had also learned English by watching American movies. I was stunned. I had not considered movies having any effects beyond providing basic entertainment value and being a source of distraction from our daily grind. Of course, with effort on their part, both students immersed themselves in the English language, which helped them to become quite fluent in both speaking and understanding a foreign language.

I had an interesting experience along these same lines recently. I was in Angola speaking at a conference. My host decided to take me on a drive around Luanda, the capital city. He stopped at a gas station to get fuel. Then a young man named Paul approached my window with a curious look. He greeted me and asked, "Sir, are you Dr. Sam Adeyemi?" He was excited when I confirmed I was indeed. He said he had found it difficult to believe that he was seeing me on the street in Luanda, but his wife had encouraged him to approach me. He pointed at his phone and said that he follows me on social media and watches a lot of my videos. I got out of the car to have a chat with him and his wife. What struck me from our conversation was his statement that he was learning to speak English from not only my videos but those of other speakers.

My point is this. What goes into a person's mind often comes out in a life experience – some good, some not so good. Just like the process model demonstrates, if you are intentional about what you see and what you hear, it will help shape your life. To recap the SHIFTS Process Model: See, Hear, Insight, Formulate, Transform, and Succeed. I encourage you to reference this model repeatedly while reading this book, apply and adapt it to your own needs in your own life, and then let your thoughts organically transform. Let the book work for you. You don't have to force anything. Discard what does not apply to you or help you, and modify anything you like. It's this personalized effort that will give you the most meaningful mind shifts. Next, assign a part, or several parts, of the easy-to-remember acronym to shifting the mindset of whatever it is you are learning, teaching others, or interested in absorbing more fully. Share it and show others how to use it.

There are a few more points I'd like to make here. In a study about the impact of film on youth, a group of children were asked to watch a Disney clip from the movie *Cars*.[5] The clip showed the main character helping another character. After the clip, those children exhibited a helping behavior toward their peers. The example they watched in the movie inspired their young minds. In another example, there has always been a great deal of controversy regarding claims that violence in movies and video games causes or leads to violent behavior. A particular study on children between the ages of 6 and 9 discovered that 15 years later, 25% of participants exposed to various content in violent television and videos were more prone to exhibit aggressive behavior in situations that could be more easily resolved with resolution skills.[6] The violent impressions made left little opportunity for recovery and redemption of a bad situation. More recent studies have established that exposure to violence on and off the screen can result in increased anxiety, as well. Mental health struggles among youth worldwide continue to soar. But I believe that if the SHIFTS model were taught in schools, many of our young people would have a tool that lifted them when they were down. Students would be able to easily recall the acronym and run through the steps for making better choices, positive decisions, and setting bolder goals that could lead them in a stronger direction. And struggles are certainly not limited to just our youth. Mental health concerns among parents, teachers, senior citizens, and young professionals continue to climb.

According to the Center for Disease Control (CDC), ADHD, anxiety and behavior problems, and depression are the most frequently diagnosed mental disorders in children. (Estimates for children ages 3–17 ever having been diagnosed in 2016–2019 prior to the Pandemic – M = million.)

ADHD 9.8% (approximately 6.0M)
Anxiety 9.4% (Approximately 5.8M)
Behavior problems 8.9% (approximately 5.5M)
Depression 4.4 % (approximately 2.7M)[7]

According to the CDC, school connectedness provided critical protection for students during COVID-19.

Statistics of percentages of children who felt connected to adults and peers at school versus children who did not feel connected:

Feelings of hopelessness (35% versus 53%)
Seriously considered attempting suicide (14% versus 26%)
Attempted suicide (6% versus 12%)
Fewer than half (47%) of youth reported feeling close to people at school during the pandemic.[8]

Psychological Well-Being and Depression

Increasingly, research is demonstrating the negative impact of screen time on the psychological well-being of children and adolescents. A large national sample (40,337) of children 2–17 years of age were evaluated in 2016 for their use of all forms of screen time.[9] Those who were exposed to more than one hour per day of screen time had "lower psychological well-being, including less curiosity, lower self-control, more distractibility, more difficulty making friends, less emotional stability, being more difficult to care for, and inability to finish tasks." Those who were 14–17 years of age who had more than seven hours a day of screen time were more than twice as likely to have been diagnosed with depression compared to those who only used screens less than one hour a day. Importantly, this study is not confounded by including

(continued)

(continued)

children with developmental or intellectual delays. In addition, it showed that the tipping point for behavioral changes seemed to occur when children were exposed to more than one hour a day of screen time.

Several studies demonstrate the relationship between increased use of screen time and depression. One longitudinal study in Denmark followed a cohort of 435 adolescents into young adulthood and found "each additional hour/day spent watching television or screen viewing in adolescence was associated with . . . greater odds of prevalent depression in young adulthood, and dose-response relationships were indicated."[10]

Another study from Canada evaluated 2482 youth in grades 7–12 and concluded, "Video game playing, and computer use, but not television viewing, was associated with more severe depressive symptoms. . . . Screen time may represent a risk factor or marker of anxiety and depression in adolescents."[11]

In a Harvard report from October 2023,
The report, "On Edge: Understanding and Preventing Young Adults' Mental Health Challenges," is based on a nationally representative survey of young adults (ages 18–25), teens, and parents conducted in December 2022. Thirty-six percent (36%) of young adults who responded to the survey reported anxiety compared to 18% of teens; 29% of young adults reported depression compared to 15% of teens.[12]

Seeing and Hearing from the Top

In David Burkus's book *Leading from Anywhere* he talks about the surge of employees working remotely and that we are fully aware that the situation for every worker is not all benefit without cost.[13] Working in solitude can have a profound and challenging effect on people's state of mind, which has been a monumental personal shift in the global workplace. So many people are already lonely at home, let alone on the job, and now they are depressed both at home and on the job. We all need to pay close attention to the cues people give us.

Leaders must keep their finger on the pulse of what's going on all around them; the better and more experienced the leader, the more intuitive they will be when initiating communications. Concern should be one of authentic care, not intrusion into someone's life, or nosiness. SHIFTS happen when leaders start to notice change early on. Shift to catching problems early and save yourself a lot of angst in the future. Ask yourself: Do you notice a fellow employee suddenly looking sad for no reason that you know of? Is he coming in late for work when he never did this before? Are you starting to spot burnout among the ranks? Do you sense more frustration or anxiety in otherwise calmer employees? Are workers acting out in a short angry burst or demonstrating lack of patience for small things? Being intuitive is a mindset. Try telling someone something mean or hurtful with a smile on your face. It's practically impossible. Your brain is sending signals that it's time to shift.

Intuition is a gift. It ranges from elation, and anticipation, and hope, to noticing possible problems before they happen,

(continued)

(continued)

and even includes natural survival instincts, like flat-out fear. It's a leader's internal compass. In his best-seller *The Gift of Fear: Survival Signals That Protect Us from Violence*, Gavin de Becker writes about trusting and acting on your intuition and points to many of the instances in the SHIFTS model. He calls his own list empowering and anxiety reducing.[14] I happen to agree.

Take a moment to think about movies, television programs, or documentaries you've watched that have influenced you and your behavior in a positive or negative manner. Which ones have been disturbing to you and cause you upset, anxiety, or questionable behavior? What movies, films, or documentaries have been a positive influence on your demeanor, your lifestyle, your understanding, career choices, and your ability to feel hope, love, and gratitude? Would you watch these movies again and again or share them with friends and family? This leads me to a helpful inexpensive tool – your personal playlist of music.

APPLICATION

Music Is Life's Playlist for Acting

Have you ever caught yourself humming a song that you did not memorize intentionally? It could be the theme song from a commercial or a song you heard at an event. This has happened to me many times. It is another demonstration of the principle that what you see and hear have the potential to enter your heart, subconsciously and consciously. There is a well-known quote attributed to Emmanuel Jal: "Music – it's the only thing that can enter your system, your mind, your heart, without your permission."[15] Emmanuel Jal is recognized for being inspiring, funny, and deeply meaningful at the same time. He leaves a mark. He's a former child soldier from South Sudan who became an international recording artist, activist, and philanthropist. Now *that's* someone who exemplifies SHIFTS! Emmanuel is the owner of Gatwitch Records, Jal Gua Foods, and founder of the Gua African charity. His world vision to help transform nations, which we discuss later in this book, is to create a higher state of consciousness and global awakening by shifting opinions, leadership styles, and every individual's self-identity. His public speaking engagements have included shared time on stage with Chris Anderson (founder of TED), his Holiness the Dalai Lama, Angelina Jolie, Richard Branson, and the Clinton Global Initiative. Emmanuel Jal is shifting mindsets and elevating people to leadership positions through the art of music, performance, and his playlist.

The influence of music on our behavior is well documented. In a 2015 study in Australia, people who actively engaged in music and dance were found to be happier than those who did not.[16] Actually, we see this globally from every walk of life. Latin communities have led the way in so many musical depictions, and thousands of other cultures worldwide have used music to heal the soul and ignite great passion. Those of us who love to watch movies are accustomed to the role music plays in communicating or evoking the emotions that go with specific scenes. This is why an Oscar at the Academy Awards ceremony is awarded to the best musical score in a movie each year. Music can make you happy or sad. It can motivate you, depress you, trigger past events, or literally leave you sobbing. When you find yourself crying in a movie theater during a movie, it's not because someone put gum under your seat. It's because the scene and the music evoked emotions deep down. When Italian tenor Andrea Bocelli sings at one of his concerts, the entire venue falls silent in awe.

Similarly, another study established that music could incite aggressive thoughts and feelings of anger.[17] Maybe it's time we become more intentional in how we process the music we listen to during our internal transformation, knowing it can help lead us to the many SHIFTS we will be faced with and make in our daily lives – and not just for ourselves but for others.

Take time to write down your life's playlist. Of course, new music enters our lives and SHIFTS our feelings, but over time, there are favorites that stick with us that we can listen to again and again because they help us to be our best in both good times and challenging times. Keep track of your life's music playlist and pay attention to the emotions you feel and how things bubble up inside of you. Write it down. Sometimes a song is just the SHIFT you've been waiting for.

Education

Education ties in tightly with the SHIFTS Transformation Model. We See (the sum of what we repeatedly see) and Hear (the sum of what you repeatedly hear) in classrooms from preschool to elementary school, middle and high schools, to the college level. We consistently see and hear people with their knowledge about law, accounting, psychology, engineering, technology, medicine, science, nutrition, and more daily. At the end, we get the approval of our school to affirm that we have grown and changed, and we have evolved to understand new ideas and, therefore, we are awarded a diploma, or a certificate of completion, Juris Doctor degree (JD), or doctoral status (PhD or MD), and many other distinctions.

Education is a powerful transformation platform. Among many scholars, it is believed to be the global solution to the poverty cycle. Research conducted by the United Nations Educational, Scientific and Cultural Organization (UNESCO) concluded that global poverty would be cut in half if most adults had at least a high school education.[18] Education SHIFTS everything. But what you do with it SHIFTS your knowledge skyward. Don't be sucked into the term *Knowledge is power.* It is not. It is the *application* of knowledge that gives you your ultimate power to shift ahead. This interpretation might seem small, but it's mighty in the result of accomplishment and mentoring others to their greater level of potential and giftedness.

Importance of Self-Education

Dedicate yourself to becoming a lifelong learner. Self-education is critical. It can shift your life circumstances faster than anything, because your awareness of the world widens, and you become exposed to all the varying possibilities that lay ahead. Certain knowledge can become outdated at a fast rate. Look at technology. Knowledge in technology changes at breakneck speed, moment to moment. And that's a good thing when you're a leader in any business. Speed counts. How does your learning cycle fit into this measure of education in today's world? There are no more excuses for not learning or trying something new. Learning is available and free to most because the internet is tailor-made to create connections between people passionate about various topics. Often, there are learning modules and experiential courses available for free in whatever field you find most beneficial. Of course, there's a limit to the credentials acquired in self-learning, but it's a great start to shifting your awareness and will count a lot when interviewing for a job or prepping a team to break all the records.

What's your plan to self-educate? When I talk about self-awareness and lifelong learning, I am not talking about an afternoon on TikTok or visiting a YouTube channel occasionally for tips on building a bookshelf in your garage. Will you go on to higher learning and grab that MBA or doctorate? It can be costly but also very worthwhile, depending on your goals and destination. Junior colleges in the United States are a critical step ladder to higher education, with excellent outcomes. University credit for experience is becoming more popular and offers precious credits for life accomplishments. Is the career path you've chosen one that changes on a dime, like politics, health care, or law? If so, how will you adapt? Remember, early on I recommended the formula to adapt, delete, modify, and expand what you learn and master. Plan and stick with it, but plan in a way that allows for flexibility when it's necessary to flex in a new direction. Notice that I've used the term *self-education*; formal education is vital, but you are the driver of your life experiences, and you should be open to SHIFTS at any level you choose – provided you have the competency. People think that the skill set itself is enough. It isn't. You must have the competence to carry out the skills you learn. When someone says to you that you can do anything you desire, that is not necessarily true. I might want to be an astronaut, but I simply do not have the competency required to execute that dream. I'm not an aviator, nor do I possess the talent for working in outer space. Competency is crucial. Focus on that, not just skill building.

Conferences and Seminars

And don't forget about attending conferences and training events, which can be rich in a wide variety of learning experiences. What will provide you with the capacity to reach your goals? What time frame will you set up to move forward? What will this transformation look like for you? Associations are also a wonderful way to self-educate. As a professional speaker I am aware of prestigious organizations, such as the US-based National Speakers Association (NSA), the nonprofit group Association for Talent Development (ATD), Toastmasters International, Society for Human Resource Management (SHRM), and many more. Almost all industries have an association, domestically and internationally. Tap into their wealth of knowledge. Go online and research which are most respected in your field and investigate participating in their learning and development initiatives. Often, programs are free of charge, or affordable to purchase. Their websites can provide a large bulk of updated learning opportunities and valuable connections. If affordability becomes a serious issue, look to volunteer at these events or submit a proposal to present if you have something to offer. In exchange for a little time and effort, you'll gain access to all the information presented at the event, without spending a dime! Get creative. Offer to barter and to present added value. Most organizers are eager to hear how they can grow their communities. Perhaps you offer to bring along four paid attendees if you get to come for free. Creativity drives SHIFTS. Lack of creativity sinks SHIFTS.

Association

There's a saying that you might be judged by the company you keep and the company you don't keep. When you are quite young, hearing this from a parent or grandparent, you might laugh at this comment, but as you age, you realize there is a lot of truth to this. People can propel your SHIFTS, or they can sink them. Here's how I know.

I was quite playful in my early years in high school and was underperforming in my academics. I had a classmate who was in the same situation. However, he made a decision that had immediate impact on his academic performance. He moved away from his friends and joined a group of best-in-class students. He went everywhere with them. Of course, his perceived *betrayal* of his old friends was the talk of the class during the new term. His decision was justified at the end of the term when his grades rose significantly into the same range as those of his new friends. That's when I realized that the people with whom you associate might affect you more than you realize. You can change the trajectory of your life by changing the people who influence you most. King Solomon, a biblical figure with a reputation for being exceptionally wise, put this concept in strong words: "Walk with the wise and become wise. Associate with fools and get in trouble."[19] Interesting point, don't you think?

The people with whom you closely associate have an outsized impact on you because you see and hear them consistently, just like we talk about in the six transformative steps to leadership. This is not a call to develop bitterness or hatred against anyone. Neither is it an encouragement to break close bonds frivolously. However, it is a call to reflect on your vision, goals, and values, and to assess whether your closest associations will take you where you want to go. It calls for courage to make tough decisions and adjustments. It's all part of elevating your leadership.

Mentoring

Mentoring ties in with the previous discussion on association, but it is worth discussing separately. Mentoring has influenced my life in remarkable ways. Mentoring is the process through which someone who has developed certain qualities or skills influences another person to develop the same qualities or skills, elevating their performance. Mentors also consistently encourage and help build necessary confidence to try new things.

> A life coach does for the rest of your life what a personal trainer does for your health and fitness.
> —Elaine MacDonald, Canadian activist

Seeing someone else achieve success breaks barriers in our minds. Something inside you tells you that if they can do it, you can do it too. Also, mentoring brings you into proximity of helpful people who will offer you a wide variety of opportunities to ask questions, clear up your doubts, dissolve assumptions, and lay hold of what really works in the area where you desire to achieve success. What really matters here is intentionality. You need to be clear about your vision, goals, and values, and to be deliberate in aligning with people who have made a similar journey and are willing to help you succeed. There's got to be a plan of action, not just a dream. In my book *Dear Leader: Your Flagship Guide to Successful Leadership*, I provide aspiring leaders with a plan for mentoring and reaching goals.[20] It includes specific goals and targeted timelines to make goals real. Top leaders support aspiring leaders. It's a great feeling to help the next generation, or a colleague, or friends to rise higher and succeed. The best mentors thrive on seeing you succeed and helping you to take that next leap of faith. They are there to help catch you when you fall and help lift you when you're down. Everyone deserves a mentor.

A simple but powerful exercise: Ask yourself who is someone you know that you would like to call your mentor? Call them. Ask for their support. How else will they know you need their help? If they cannot carve out the time, they most likely will know of someone else who can assist. They might have resources or suggestions that will help you to make the most significant SHIFTS in your life. Here's a secret. You don't have to know the person. Some mentors can be great examples from afar, even if you never meet in person. What do you need to do to connect with them? Social media is a fantastic way to connect with potential mentors. It's easy to follow the top leaders you aspire to be like. Often they post information that is very helpful. A great example to me is American author, executive coach, and speaker Marshall Goldsmith. He recently announced he was stepping back from his coaching practice and offered all of his tips, tools, and techniques free of charge to anyone interested in becoming successful like he has done. What a self-effacing gift – a top-notch author and coach willing to share everything he has for free! It doesn't get any better than this. But even with such generosity, an aspiring student must take the first step to move toward the opportunity at hand. When will you take the first step?

And, in the connected world, you might be able to do more than just passively follow your mentors from afar. You'd be surprised at the number of genuinely accomplished, famous people who are generous enough to respond earnestly to a direct message or email! Executives, authors, and leaders are often so passionate about their areas of expertise that they'll respond to thoughtful comments or questions, even from complete strangers. I know one person whose nine-year-old daughter watched a documentary on income inequality featuring Robert Reich, who served as Bill Clinton's

Secretary of Labor. She had questions after the film, so on her father's advice, she tracked down an email address through Google and sent them to Reich, who responded less than two days later with thoughtful answers and suggestions for further reading. Like I said: You'd be surprised how willing even very successful people are to talk about the fields they care about – but after all, it was that love of the topic that made them successful in the first place!

Exposure

My first trip from Africa to Europe was for a family vacation with Nike and our children. We visited Greece and then Italy. This was long before it became super easy to make a hotel reservation on your phone for somewhere halfway around the world. Although we had a reservation for a hotel in Athens, Greece, we did not have one for Milan. We bought a tourist guide for Milan while in Athens and saw the addresses and phone numbers for hotels. We used airport phones to make reservations at two hotels when we landed in Milan. One hotel was low budget; the other was a five-star hotel. We took a taxi to the low-budget hotel. To our surprise, there was only one staff member on duty. She checked us in, and then explained that some people would join her to serve breakfast only in the mornings. She then led us to the elevator. It looked so old. She explained that the elevator could not take our bags and us at once. So we would go first, then press the button for the ground floor to send the elevator back to her. We did so. Then she moved our bags into the elevator and pressed the button for our floor to send our bags to us. I was having a sinking feeling already. When we entered our room, my mood sank completely. I told Nike, "We're not staying here."

Let me explain what was going through my mind. I saw the trip to Europe as an opportunity for our minds to absorb a more beautiful environment than we had ever been accustomed to. This hotel was even lower in quality than what we had expected. However, there was a slight limitation to the idea of changing hotels. We had limited funds. If we stayed at the low-budget hotel, we would have some money for shopping. If we stayed at the five-star hotel, there would be no money left for shopping. Nike and I decided we were moving to the five-star hotel. Absorbing pictures and memories that would shift our minds for a lifetime was of higher priority than shopping. I went downstairs to inform the hotel staff of our decision. She was gracious and helped to call a taxi. The moment we arrived at the five-star hotel, we were welcomed by smartly dressed porters and a lively and beautiful environment. We were happy with our decision.

Let me emphasize that staying at a low-budget hotel is not a bad decision, depending on your circumstances. This decision was made based on our vision of transformation and the knowledge that whatever we saw and heard while on that vacation was going to stay with us and help us to experience a shift in our status.

The human mind functions like a camera. The eye is your aperture, the small hole through which light enters the camera to establish an image on the memory card or film. It is this image on the memory card or film that is printed out later as a photograph. Likewise, life has a way of printing the images on your mind into reality. To change those images, be intentional about what you see. You might even need to invest in yourself and environments that will help you absorb new images into your mental memory card. This sets the vision and future of what is yet to come.

When You Shift to See and Hear You Build Competencies

Webster's Dictionary defines competency or competence as possessing a wide base of knowledge or experience for a specified purpose. But in our workplace, competency can have many more meanings, like values, humor, technical skills, and so on. This is where the term *attribute bundle* comes from. It's a collection of competencies. Whether it's a bundle of attributes or a single competency, they've got to link with the organization's overall goals and objectives if they are to shift people upward.

How do I fit in? We all share a common need. We need to know where we fit in and where we are accepted so that we too can succeed and perform at our best. So how do we apply the competencies we learn over time to make it easier for people to fit into our groups, our tribes, and our communities?

 Exercise Aligning Leadership Competencies with Group Integration

EXERCISE 1

Objective: To help you and your team members understand how core leadership competencies can be applied to foster inclusivity, collaboration, and a sense of belonging within your groups, tribes, and communities.

INSTRUCTIONS

Identify Core Competencies: Start by reviewing the list of leadership competencies provided here. These competencies are essential for building a cohesive and high-performing team.

　　Trust and values

　　Integrity

(continued)

(continued)

Deep listening

Team building

Passion and intuition

Competitive spirit

Decision-making

Humor and enthusiasm

Agile change and adaptability

Vision

Personal Reflection: Take a few minutes to reflect on each competency. Consider how these competencies currently manifest in your leadership style and how they influence the dynamics within your team or community. For each competency, ask yourself the following:

How do I demonstrate this competency in my daily interactions?

How does this competency contribute to the overall success and harmony of my team?

Team Discussion: Organize a team meeting or workshop where each member will discuss these competencies. Begin by explaining the importance of each competency and how it contributes to creating a sense of belonging and high performance within the group.

Ask each team member to share their thoughts on how these competencies apply to their roles. Encourage them to provide examples from their own experiences.

Application Exercise: For each competency, have the team discuss the following:

> **Definition:** What does this competency mean in the context of our team?
>
> **Importance:** Why is this competency crucial for building a strong, inclusive team?
>
> **Implementation:** How can we apply this competency in our daily work? What actions or behaviors can we adopt to embody this competency more fully?

After discussing each competency, ask the team to identify specific actions they can take to reinforce these competencies in their interactions.

Action Plan Development: Collaboratively develop an action plan where each team member commits to practicing specific competencies. For example, someone might commit to improving "deep listening" by actively practicing reflective listening in meetings.

Set a timeline for when these actions will be implemented and schedule follow-up meetings to discuss progress and challenges.

Ongoing Review and Adjustment: Regularly revisit these competencies in team meetings. Discuss what's working, what isn't, and how the team can continue to evolve.

Encourage an open dialogue where team members feel comfortable sharing their experiences and adjustments they've made to better integrate these competencies into their work.

Outcome: This exercise will help each team member understand their role in fostering a positive, inclusive

(continued)

(continued)

environment by aligning their personal actions with key leadership competencies. The exercise also encourages ongoing self-reflection and team dialogue, which are essential for continuous improvement and collective success.

STUMBLING BLOCKS

Stumbling Blocks and Strategies to Overcome Them

1. Avoid Being Nonspecific

Stumbling Block: Lack of specificity can cause confusion and hinder progress within a team or organization. When goals, expectations, or feedback are vague, it becomes challenging for people to know exactly what is expected of them.

Strategy to Overcome: Always strive for clarity in communication. Define goals, roles, and tasks with precision. Provide concrete examples and clear guidelines to ensure everyone understands their responsibilities and how to achieve them. Specificity helps to create a focused path forward, enabling team members to shift their efforts in the right direction and achieve better outcomes.

2. Set People Up for Success, Not Failure

Stumbling Block: Assigning tasks or responsibilities without proper support or resources can set team members up for failure, leading to frustration and decreased morale.

Strategy to overcome: Before delegating tasks, evaluate the resources, tools, and training necessary for success. Ensure that each team member has what they need to accomplish their goals. By providing the right support, you empower your team to succeed, which fosters confidence and encourages continuous improvement.

3. Hire for Competency, Not Just Specific Skills

Stumbling Block: Focusing solely on specific skill sets during the hiring process can lead to overlooking candidates who have the potential to grow and excel in a dynamic environment.

Strategy to Overcome: Prioritize hiring for competency and potential. Look for candidates who demonstrate adaptability, problem-solving skills, and a willingness to learn. These qualities often prove more valuable in the long run than a narrow set of technical skills. By hiring individuals who are competent and capable of growth, you build a more resilient and versatile team.

4. Be Transparent, Not Vague

Stumbling Block: Vague communication can lead to misunderstandings and mistrust within a team. When leaders are not transparent, it creates uncertainty and can erode confidence.

Strategy to Overcome: Practice transparency in all communications. Be open about the reasoning behind decisions, provide clear answers to questions, and foster an environment where team members feel informed and valued. Transparency builds trust and ensures that everyone is on the same page, which is crucial for effective collaboration and leadership.

What We See and Hear Develops Competency Levels: Consistently expose yourself and your team to positive visual and auditory inputs to build strong leadership competencies.

Visual and Auditory Practices Galvanize Talents: Use vision boards, affirmations, and other practices to reinforce goals and drive success.

Support Growth with Workable Tools: Equip your team with the necessary resources and tools to succeed, ensuring they can perform at their best.

Listen More Than You Speak: Cultivate deep listening within your team to understand their needs and perspectives, which will enhance decision-making and team cohesion.

Foster Inclusivity: Make every effort to help people feel they are part of something bigger. Inclusion and diversity are vital for a thriving, innovative team.

By being mindful of these stumbling blocks and actively working to overcome them, you can create an environment where both individuals and the team as a whole can thrive, making the necessary shifts for continued growth and success.

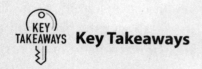 **Key Takeaways**

In this chapter, we've explored the profound influence of what we see and hear on our subconscious mind and, ultimately, our leadership journey. By intentionally curating your visual and auditory environment, you can harness the power of these sensory inputs to shape your mindset, reinforce your goals, and drive your actions. The images you consistently expose yourself to – whether through vision boards or other visual aids – embed deeply within your subconscious, influencing your beliefs and behaviors in ways that propel you toward success.

Similarly, the words and sounds you allow into your daily environment hold immense power. Positive messages, affirmations, and associations with uplifting voices all contribute to fostering a mindset primed for growth. By surrounding yourself with these empowering influences, you create the conditions for sustained leadership development and transformation.

As we move forward, remember that transformation begins with what you see and hear. By being intentional about these inputs, you can set the stage for the next steps in your leadership evolution, enabling your vision to become reality and driving your journey toward personal and professional success.

Chapter 3

Insights and Formulate

Harnessing Insights to Formulate Impactful Strategies

In this chapter, we delve into two critical components of the SHIFTS model: Insights and Formulate. These elements are essential for understanding how leaders can internalize new perspectives and convert them into actionable strategies.

Insights are the foundation of innovation, enabling us to perceive patterns, connect the dots, and generate solutions that go beyond surface-level understanding. It's about developing a deeper inner vision that helps you make sense of complex situations and prepares you for strategic decision-making. Through insights, we learn to create mental models that will guide our actions and empower us to shape reality.

Formulate, however, represents the process of translating these insights into tangible decisions and actions. It's the stage where internal change happens, where beliefs are solidified, and new strategies are crafted. This chapter will explore how to move from simply understanding an idea to making decisive, impactful choices that align with your goals and aspirations.

By the end of this chapter, you'll gain a comprehensive understanding of how to tap into your inner insights to guide innovative thinking, and how to formulate actionable plans that lead to sustainable success. You will learn practical strategies for gathering insights from varied experiences, applying those insights to real-world challenges, and making decisions that drive continuous growth and improvement. Expect to come away with both the mindset and tools to lead with creativity and purpose, enabling SHIFTS that foster both personal and organizational transformation.

How Insights Help Us Focus on Change

One of our managers made an unusual request one day. She was in charge of managing the facilities for our company, which also managed most of our companies' sites in Nigeria. What her team needed to reach a five-star goal was find a way to examine bigger, more successful projects, which were very limited then in Nigeria. The team approached the manager and requested to travel to the United Arab Emirates, a much more bustling business environment, where they could meet with construction experts, architects, and other facilities managers to benchmark exciting new building projects. They offered to pay for half of their own expenses if our company would cover the other half. The proposal seemed intriguing and reasonable. The team was so hungry to learn and expand their thinking that they were willing to invest in themselves.

I approved the team manager's request because she had a clear idea of the impact the trip would have on her team. Previously, I had encouraged her personally to go on vacation to the UAE with her family, to gain a fresh perspective and examine global ideas she could return with and help others to learn from. She had done so, and came back a different person.

She immediately changed several processes in our office that proved to be profitable and progressive. Just like the SHIFTS model in this book, she saw and heard things that entered her heart, transformed her internal ideas, and expanded her personal limitations. She shifted her team upward with a new sense of creativity and zest. Isn't that what all leaders want to see happen? I was thrilled, to say the least. And now, that individual experience had branched out to affect her entire team – so I was happy to sign off on the trip.

The previous chapter was about our vision – our literal sight of the physical world we encounter, and the ways we can manipulate the images we allow in to shift our future reality. This chapter turns within to discuss our metaphorical vision: our insight. Have you ever been in a discussion when you were struggling to understand what the other party was communicating, and then, suddenly, you got it and exclaimed, "Oh, I see"? You were not referring to your physical eyesight. You were referring to your inner eyes on the world.

Insight is the ability to see with our inner eyes. We can see with our minds – with our imagination. Our inner eyes are critical to our ability to translate intangible realities into tangible reality. What we see with our inner eye is what we eventually see with our physical eyes. If someone's inner eye is functioning, but their physical eyes are not working, they still have high chances of achieving success in life. However, if someone's physical eyes are functioning, but their inner eye is not, it will be difficult for them to make a success of any opportunity.

Insights help us to understand what is happening, why it's happening, and what makes each event different from other things that have happened. It helps us to establish cause-and-effect connections, leading to better decisions and better

Insights and Formulate

control of situations. Once we're able to establish the effect or result that we want, we understand how to cause it to happen.

Insights help us to connect dots and identify patterns. They help us to detect the principle that is controlling an experience. Understanding the principle empowers us to re-create the experience, because *principles make success predictable.* In fact, understanding a principle fuels our creativity as we explore possible ways to leverage the power of that principle to solve various problems. Insights help mental creation, and mental creation precedes physical creation.

Inspired by Insights

A little over 30 years ago, someone invited me to his home to watch a video presentation by Dr. Myles Munroe, who was a speaker, author, leadership consultant, and minister. The presentation had a profound effect on me. The depth of insights created the effect. It was eye-opening and paradigm shifting. I was deep in thought as I watched. I went beyond enjoying the presentation and began to earnestly desire a personal transformation. I wanted to be able to teach with such insight in my presentations. So, as I listened, I was processing everything in my mind. I thought, "How is this man able to communicate like this?" My mind yielded an answer: "This man was not born this way; he became like this. And if he became like this, I can become like this, too." I am still on the journey of transformation that began that day. However, I have come a long way, always shifting in a positive direction toward my goals. As I watched Munro on the screen, I watched something amazing with my physical eyes, moved the scenario into my imagination, and began to reach insight into how I could become like the speaker. Insights move you from *information* to *understanding.*

What You See Isn't Always What You Get

My training as an engineer influences the way I look at buildings. There is a part that is visible to the eye, and there is a part that is not. We call the invisible part the *substructure*. It determines the limit of what the visible part, the superstructure, can do. I'm applying here my hobby of breaking up English words, like *understanding*, and I get two words: *under* and *standing*. So, understanding implies the ability to gain insight into what is under the thing that is standing. As the SHIFTS Process Model tells us, your insight and feelings anchor your beliefs about yourself and the world. You need to set apart time to think, reflect, pray or meditate, and then to mentally digest information, to gain understanding. Once you grasp the principle that controls an experience, you can re-create that experience over and over. This brings me to the point that leadership success is a process, a hard-won understanding that we intentionally repeat. Success is simply a repeat performance of what you've done before, with each new iteration getting better and better as you near your ultimate goal. The circumstances might change over time, but the underlying process remains quite similar.

It was through my meditations that I established the belief that money has not always been in existence. Back in the days, people did trade by barter. The important thing was that you brought something of value to the market so you could make an exchange. That led to my decision to always offer products and services that are of value to people. This is a realistic way to attract money. I have come to realize that we can get insights from all kinds of situations, both the good and the bad. It's how we respond and not react to each situation that sets leaders apart.

The Value of Insights

Insights lead to solutions. They lead to innovative ideas that solve tangible problems. They help us understand why we are not getting the results we desire and guide us in creating pathways for applying information to our peculiar circumstances or the peculiar circumstances of our customers.

Insights inspire. They activate our emotions, making their occurrences such distinct experiences that we can easily recollect. They cause the release of dopamine in the brain, giving pleasure.

Insights increase efficiency. They can save time and money, both in our personal and organizational lives.

Insights can lead to the creation of products and services.

We are more likely to act on our insights. They help us to own the solutions we are acting on. Moreover, understanding helps the application of a principle.

How to Get Insights

Mohanbir Sawhney and Sanjay Khosla outlined seven insight channels that innovators can use in a *Harvard Business Review* article titled "Where to Look for Insight."[1] They are anomalies (things that deviate from the norm), confluence (the points where trends combine to create new opportunities), frustrations (the things that create deficiencies in your systems and processes), orthodoxies (the assumptions, beliefs, and behaviors that have been unchallenged), extremities (the process of learning from the behaviors and needs of the best and the worst employees and customers), voyages (the process of learning through immersion in a different context, especially the sociocultural contexts of your employees or customers), and analogies (the ability to adapt successful methods and strategies into new contexts where they haven't yet been tried). In addition to focusing on these seven insight channels, it's beneficial to cultivate the habits of reflection and meditation. Research has confirmed that reflection separates exceptional professionals from ordinary ones.[2] As you brood on what you have seen and heard, you identify what worked, what didn't work, who made it work, and the cause-and-effect relationships between actions and results. You gain clarity about how to achieve your goals.

Getting out of work mode can unlock wonders in finding new insights. I have received tons of ideas in the shower and while on vacation. This is because when you focus intensely on a problem, your brain will continue working on it, like software running in your computer background, even when you're otherwise occupied. I had an insight in this way once while on vacation to the UAE with my wife, and the resulting implementation enabled one of our organizations to double in size over three months. I received the next big idea in the shower shortly after, which resulted in our doubling in size again over another four months. We capture insights more easily when there is little neural activity. Insights create SHIFTS in our belief system, and these new beliefs lead us to make new decisions.

Like my team manager, and the team she eventually carried to the UAE in search of new avenues for company growth, each of us has the ability to enable our physical observation of the world around us shape our inner lives. In a positive feedback loop, these new insights begin to shape the world around us to match the vision we've let in – and the process can repeat, over and over again, for as long as we allow it.

Insights and Formulate

Formulate

As we move from the realm of Insights to Formulate, we transition from understanding to action. Insights offer us a new lens to view the world, enabling us to recognize patterns and opportunities that might not have been visible before. But the value of insight lies in what we do with it.

This is where Formulate comes in – it's the process of converting those newfound perspectives into actionable decisions. Formulation bridges the gap between internal understanding and external execution, ensuring that insights don't remain abstract ideas but become the foundation for strategic actions that lead to growth and transformation. In this next section, we will explore how to channel the power of insights into decision-making processes that drive consistent, tangible results.

I will illustrate this as I complete my story about the first time I watched Dr. Myles Munroe on video. After gaining the insight that he was not born packed with phenomenal insights, but rather became that way through intentional practice, I applied the insight to my life. He was speaking at a church conference and a lot of his insights were from the scriptures. So I said, "I will never read my Bible passively again." Actually, I have applied that decision to my study life generally. When I read a book, I star or underline the sentences that yield insights for me. Sometimes I make double lines for emphasis. And, sometimes, I make notes beside a sentence or paragraph, because an idea in the book has sparked off a new idea in my mind. Some of those notes then become actions I decide to take.

We form new beliefs when we gain new insights. We make decisions based on our new beliefs. Some of those decisions are deep. They are decisions about who we are. We change our self-image. It's like overhauling the foundation of a building, giving it capacity to carry more floors. To achieve new results with consistency, we need to become who we have not been before. We formulate new dimensions to our lives by making decisions. This is the stage of internal change in our SHIFTS model.

A study conducted by University of Chicago economist Steven Levitt found that people who made decisions for change, rather than choosing to maintain the status quo, were more satisfied with their decisions and were happier six months down the line.[3] When you make decisions in alignment with your new dreams, goals, and beliefs, you experience internal change. You become the version of yourself that you've idealized in your vision. That version of you will attract everything and everyone in your vision. It's like putting more power in a magnet. You can now attract people, resources, and opportunities that you could not attract before. Your decision is now beginning to determine your destiny.

Goals with Deadlines

One of the insights that influenced me on decision-making was the story of Dr. Frank Gunsaulus as told by Napoleon Hill in *Think and Grow Rich*.[4] Dr. Gunsaulus had the vision to build a school in the state of Illinois, and for two years he described the school he would build if he could raise a million dollars. But one Friday, a thought came into his mind: "When will you get the million dollars?" He decided there and then that he would find a way to raise the money in two weeks. He said afterwards that it was as if the universe had been waiting for him to make that decision. A simple idea occurred to him: that he should make that his sermon that Sunday. He put a notice in a newspaper on Saturday that he would be speaking on the

Insights and Formulate

topic, "What I Would Do If I Had a Million Dollars." He delivered the sermon on Sunday; afterward, a man walked up and invited Gunsaulus to visit his office on Monday. At that Monday meeting, Dr. Gunsaulus received a check for $1 million – all stemming from a simple, time-bound decision to do a certain thing by a firm deadline.

There is power in a made-up mind. Things don't become dynamic in our world until they become specific. Decision-making helps us to be specific with our goals and with the deadlines for achieving them. People who make up their minds are generally more successful than those who don't make up their minds. Invisible forces seem to come to the aid of those who make up their minds.

- Decision-making builds our self-confidence.
- Decision-making helps us to hold steady in the face of challenges.
- Decision-making helps us to form new habits. It might be to read more frequently, exercise more, or to invest in relationships.
- Decision-making helps people around us to be aware of the changes going on in our lives and to adjust to our new priorities.
- Decision-making activates your creativity.

How to Make Decisions

Minimize your options. Apply the Pareto Principle, which suggests that 20% of what you do gives you 80% of your results. Eliminate the 80% of activity that is less efficient and it becomes easier to make all future decisions. Similarly, eliminate the least desirable options and you will get better clarity with the options that are left. Get advice, but also minimize feedback. Listening to too many people can leave you confused.

Practice making up your mind quickly with small decisions, that don't have big consequences. They say too much analysis leads to paralysis.

Hold firmly to your decision and don't change for as long as possible, except if there are compelling reasons. Learn to trust your intuition or your inner voice. It usually comes to you first even before you get all the facts. Life is not always linear.

Make decisions when you are fully rested and calm. Anxiety can distort the brain's function.

 EXERCISE **Exercise Practicing Intentional Meditation**

Objective: To develop a personal practice of consistent meditation that will guide you in bringing your vision to reality.

INSTRUCTIONS
Select a Reading: If you're focused on spiritual growth, this might be a passage of scripture or a meaningful devotional work. If you're focused on leadership or business, this might be a book chapter, article, blog post, or podcast connected to your goals.
Identify a Core Message: As you read (or listen), take notes or annotations on the things that "catch your mind." Don't stop reading to mull them over in the moment; the goal

(continued)

(continued)

here is to get through the content while culling out the parts that are likely to be useful over time.

Review and "Crop the Picture": As you read over your notes later, select a single point that you'd like to truly internalize. (Don't throw the rest away! You might come back to them later for the same process.) Just as we crop a picture to isolate the truly fascinating part of an image, you are cropping a set of ideas down to its most useful essence for this particular moment.

Reflect, Reflect, Reflect: Literally. Write the message you've selected on a card, or use an online design tool to make an image out of it. Place it next to your mirror, where you'll be guaranteed to see it twice a day, as you prepare in the morning and evening. You might even take a picture of it and make it your phone background, for further emphasis. Leave it up for at least a week, but leave it up until you're satisfied that the message is sufficiently internalized that it's beginning to yield true insight, even when it's not directly in your field of vision.

Results: You'll find over time that the principle you've selected begins popping up, unbidden and automatically, as you are making decisions. You'll begin having true insight, seeing connections to the principle in places you might not otherwise have found them, simply because you've intentionalized the process of imprinting a valuable principle on your consciousness. When you feel it's sufficiently ingrained, select another reading (or another principle from your first reading), and repeat this process.

EXERCISE 1

Exercise Iterative Decision-Making for Groups

Objective: To help you and your team navigate a decision, allowing Insight to guide the way.

INSTRUCTIONS

Choose a Topic: Select an upcoming decision your team will face for this exercise. It's important that it be far enough away to not need instant action, but close enough to create a sense of low-level urgency. And, for your first attempt, don't select something that's critical to the life or health of the organization; save that for when your team has developed comfort with the process.

Frame the Decision: In a group setting, outline the question at hand. For example, it might be a question about the best way to market an upcoming business offering. As the leader, identify the primary outcome desired by the decision, but don't suggest potential courses of action to get there.

Collect First Thoughts: Ask each member of the group to submit two to three initial, gut-level ideas on paper or via a digital platform. Allow just enough time for them to absorb the issue, formulate initial responses, and submit them. Then dismiss the meeting, telling them you'll follow up.

Distribute and Consider: The next day, send the team a document containing each suggestion in alphabetical order, along with a related case study, journal article, or comparable material from another company. Ask them to read it carefully, then let it percolate until the next meeting.

(continued)

Insights and Formulate

(continued)

Rank and Cut: A few days later, reconvene the group, and list each item at the front of the room. Give each member four sticky notes for voting, and tell them they can distribute them however they want: all four on a single idea, one vote on four separate ideas, or any other combination. However, once everyone has voted, the bottom 80% are getting cut. Once you've cut the list down to 20%, dismiss the meeting.

Reflect and Tweak: After the meeting, communicate to the team the list of the top 20% ideas. Ask them to think about them in light of the article you'd previously asked them to read and come prepared to propose changes before the group finalizes a plan at the next meeting.

Discuss and Decide: When the group meets again, the ideas you've seeded them with and the insights they arrived at independently are likely to lead to connections and possibilities no one saw initially, and you should be able to leave this meeting with a firm plan of action in place that enjoys true group consensus. If not, you can simply keep repeating the vote-cut-tweak process until a winning plan emerges.

STUMBLING BLOCKS Stumbling Blocks and Strategies to Overcome Them

1. Lack of Imagination

Stumbling Block: Many teams, especially in long-term organizations that aren't in immediate danger, unconsciously adopt a bias toward established processes. "What exists has worked so far, so it's likely to keep working well enough forever," they think.

And they might be right! But no one has ever said their organizational dream was "working well enough." To achieve and maintain excellence, teams must always be willing to evaluate and refine (or throw overboard) what currently exists.

Strategy to Overcome: Two questions are useful here: "What if it wasn't?" and "What might make it even better?"

It's important to periodically sit down as a group, write down a sentence that the organization has (consciously or unconsciously) begun treating as an infallible truth, and ask these questions.

What if this wasn't the maximum possible profit margin on that service or product? What if that sector of the industry weren't closed off to new competition? What if grading weren't the best way to communicate competency to our students? What exists that we're not seeing because we've adopted a framework whose boundaries we no longer even think about exploring?

2. Decision Paralysis

Stumbling Block: Occasionally, decisions become so daunting that we can't process the options enough to make one, and we become trapped in an infinite loop of consideration and reconsideration, weighing each pro and con until we reach an equilibrium whose default is "keep doing nothing."

Strategy to Overcome: In this situation, one way to break the logjam is to choose ALL the options. Obviously, this isn't a realistic outcome. But one way to reach new insight is simple: However many options there are, choose that many people you trust. Imagine you have three potential

83

Insights and Formulate

solutions to a difficult problem. Write each one down on a separate card, and put all three cards in a box.

Now, select three people you trust to give solid advice on the matter. Begin composing an email to person A, and draw one of the three choices from the box. Make the best case possible to explain why you might choose that route, and ask them to consider it and give their feedback before you finalize anything. Repeat the process two more times, and you'll get three honest assessments that might contain pros and cons you hadn't considered. In addition, while you're waiting for their responses, the problem will continue to churn in the background. Often, this is enough to break the logjam and make the best path forward clear.

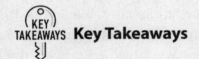 **Key Takeaways**

As we conclude our exploration of Insights and Formulate, we have learned how to harness new perspectives and transform them into strategic actions. Insights provide clarity, and formulation ensures those insights lead to meaningful decisions that drive growth. Now, we turn our attention to the next phase of the SHIFTS model: Transform and Succeed. In this upcoming chapter, we will dive into how transformation is achieved by consistently applying the insights we've gained and how success is measured by the lasting impact of these transformations. Together, Transform and Succeed will reveal how to create lasting change and realize the full potential of our shifts. Let's explore the steps that ensure these changes lead to true success, both personally and professionally.

Chapter 4

Transform and Succeed

The Path to Transformation and Success

In this chapter, we'll discuss a basic reality about Transformation: the idea that changing the physical world requires concrete, physical action. We'll move on to discuss the idea that because success isn't stagnant, we can never rest on our laurels and stop growing.

By the end of the chapter, you'll be ready to take a look at the exercises that will help you transform ideas into actions, and you'll learn which stumbling blocks are likely to crop up and how best to avoid them.

Let's start the transformation process.

Transform

I often say in my presentations that colleges do not have a PhD program for "Planning to Study Chemistry." Our world does not recognize you for what you are planning to do but for what you have done. A friend works with a teacher who is famous on his campus for the mantra "I can't grade what you *meant* to do; I can only grade what you *did*." The SHIFTS message emphasizes the need for sustainable change to start from the mind. However, you can't live out a dream that remains in your mind; you need action orientation to bring your invisible realities into physical manifestation. There is a legendary statement that says, "Nothing ventured, nothing gained." I figure that many of us are much more successful in the intangible world than we are in the material world. Sadly, this gap between our inner and outer realities creates frustration. Developing the habit of acting on your plans separates you from the crowd. It makes you a creator. You make things happen, rather than waiting for things to happen.

My team hosted our C-suite leadership retreat in Marrakech, Morocco, recently. We had a layover at Casablanca. Some of the passengers approached me as we walked to our boarding gate for the flight to Marrakech. They asked to confirm that I was really Sam Adeyemi, explaining that they were from Gambia and had been greatly inspired by my radio and TV broadcast, *Success Power*. We ran the two broadcasts on national radio and TV some years ago. My manager was informed by the TV station that, once, their former president had been watching *Success Power* and had called the station to instruct them to repeat our broadcast for the whole country to watch. (Gambia is not a large country and the president was more of an autocrat.) I was welcomed like a rock star the first time I visited Gambia, with journalists from the national television station waiting to interview me on arrival at the airport, even though we arrived at about 1 a.m. When I reflect on the impact of *Success Power*, I ask myself, "What if I had not started?"

I founded two organizations in 1995: Success Power International and Daystar Christian Centre. Both were the product of an inspired idea. It took a lot of daring to launch them. The first to start was Success Power and our first product was a radio broadcast. I had no idea how to go about creating a radio show, but I announced it at a meeting anyway. Two gentlemen walked up to me, introduced themselves, and went on to play phenomenal roles in birthing that dream. They were professionals in the media and advertising worlds. At the time, I didn't have the required communication skills, but they coached me. I also had no idea where the funds would come from, but when people learned of my plans, the funds began to roll in. Finally, I didn't think I was qualified to teach people how to succeed because I was 27 and didn't think I had accomplished much at that point. Like most people, I underestimated the value that I had to add to people's lives. For example, I had already read more books at that age than most people read in a lifetime: hundreds of them. The broadcast was a hit from the first episode. Today, I meet people in many places whose lives have been transformed through Success Power. I am absolutely grateful that I dared to start, rather than allowing it to remain a wish for someday.

Why You Should Take Action

Thoughts do not impact the physical world until they become actions. It is action that leads to accomplishments. One of Newton's Laws of Motion suggests that all objects remain at a state of rest until a force is applied. This implies that things don't move themselves in our world. We need to move them. Likewise, goals don't achieve themselves. It is up to you to make them happen. There is a measure of pleasure that comes with the accomplishment of a goal, and the intensity depends on the size or importance of the goal. These boosts give your life a sense of purpose and meaning, especially if you are adding value to yourself and others. Achieving goals is the way you turn your internal SHIFTS into reality in the material world.

Action often has a cumulative effect, speeding up your subsequent learning and growth. You never know what is waiting

87

Transform and Succeed

on the other side of your action. You experience miracles sometimes. What seems difficult before you try might turn out to be surprisingly easy. You will likely meet people who will be catalysts for the accomplishment of your goals. You might gain access to resources that were not available before you took action. I have experienced all these. But probably the greatest benefit you get is the shift of your knowledge as it moves from theory to experiential, and the new person you become as a result.

Action builds your confidence. As you discover what works and what doesn't, your probability for achieving success increases with each new venture. You increasingly overcome fear and doubts. Eventually, you are recognized as an expert in your field.

Action helps you to change your habits, which are fundamental to your ability to achieve goals. Many do not accomplish their goals because their habits frustrate their intentions. You can't wish bad habits away. You can only replace them, and you do so through consistent action.

Action helps us to build momentum. In introductory physics classes, we learn that the coefficient of friction is larger for a stationary object than an object that is already moving. Simply put, it's easier to keep a moving object going than it is to put something stationary into motion. Inertia is the tendency for an object to do what it's already doing, the force that keeps stationary things where they are. So, because there are forces trying to keep you stationary in life, you need to apply massive action to get yourself moving. Then continuous action will keep you moving.

As you develop action orientation, start with aligning your vocabulary with your vision. Words are like seeds. They convey intangible realities to our material world. The realities of your life today are likely harvests from the seeds you sowed with your mouth yesterday. As you shift your mindset, also shift the things you say to align with the new you. For example, if you are now wealthy internally, with an abundance mindset, don't talk as if there is scarcity everywhere else. Change how you refer to yourself. Practice this until it becomes a habit. Author James Clear says in *Atomic Habits* that we should take small actions first, achieve consistency in taking them, and then scale up.[1]

Finally, on this point, make efforts to overcome procrastination and act with persistence. Waiting to reflect before you act has its advantages. It can improve the quality of your decisions. But don't wait too long. Don't let waiting become a habit. I had to reprogram my mind in this area. I took sheets of plain paper and wrote "Do it now" 1,000 times. Those words were ingrained in my mind and they jump at me and prompt me to take action today. Then, always remember that things don't always work out the first time. It takes repeated action to achieve success. I was amazed several years back when I learned the generally accepted rule that 80% of sales are made between the 5th and 12th calls. I was used to moving on after the first attempt. My success rate jumped as I learned to be more persistent. Take persistent action and you will experience big jumps in your results.

Succeed

You have found what works. Now, work more on it. Success is repetitive in nature. It is habitual. Learning to drive is literally cultivating new habits of coordinated activities. After some time, driving becomes second nature – something we do automatically, without much cognitive load. It's the same with success. The principles that govern success and leadership don't change. Continue to satisfy their requirements and you are likely to be succeeding in the long term. However, you must bear in mind that circumstances and people change. You will therefore need to continuously adapt principles to changing situations. This will enable you to move from experiencing one SHIFT to experiencing multiple SHIFTS.

Change Is Inevitable

The first time I read *Who Moved My Cheese* by Spencer Johnson,[2] I found it so helpful that I went through it with all our staff at one of our organizations. Johnson's story of two men and two mice trapped in a maze, craving the cheese they love so much, first drives home the principle that someone will always be moving your cheese. In other words, change always happens. Smart people don't wait for change to happen to them; they sense change before it happens, determine their response, and leverage change to accelerate their success. You see crisis as opportunities, not as problems, when you have a leadership mindset. You need to be strategic, being aware of your strengths and opportunities, and leveraging them for outsized results. At the same time, you need to be aware of your weaknesses and areas of vulnerability, and to prepare against potential losses or destruction. I encourage you to go beyond planning that assumes only single or stable scenarios to doing scenario planning, envisaging several best and worst possible scenarios, and to prepare for as many as possible. I do this with CEOs at the beginning of every year. It minimizes surprises, and many go on to accelerate success for their organizations during crisis times.

Reinvent

You need to scale up several times to be able to achieve your ultimate vision. This requires that you repeat the SHIFTS process. When you've been at a particular level of success for some time, it's natural that your soul begins to crave more. The environment around you is changing every day and you have to jog along to maintain your position. But to make big jumps forward, you need to become a new person again. You need to reinvent yourself. I have had to do this several times, and I appreciate why many people don't do it. The current you will need to "die" for the new you to emerge, figuratively. You need to let go of what you've believed to learn new things. For example, this is what you experience when you let go of your 9–5 job to pursue your dreams as an entrepreneur. You shift from being an employee to becoming an employer. Even as a business owner, you will likely start as the employer and employee at the same time. You will need a new mindset to bring people in and to delegate work to them while shifting your role to that of supervisor or manager. Exercise courage, let go of the old you, run through the SHIFTS process again, and shift your success and influence to a new level.

Succession

None of us is going to be here forever. This is true not only for our existence in this world but also for most of our roles. Don't define your success only by what happens when you occupy a role. Think beyond your time. Think of how the SHIFTS will continue after you have left. The best time to begin to think about it is the moment you begin to occupy the role. Recruit with succession in mind. Identify people with the potential to occupy the role. Value the development of potential leaders. Invest in them, and leave when it's time. Don't let insecurity prevent you from empowering others. When you let go of your current level of success, it frees you to move higher.

EXERCISE **Exercise Thinking Backwards**

Objective: To help you create an actionable list of concrete steps that move you incrementally toward your ultimate goal.

INSTRUCTIONS

Choose Your Frustration: Select something you're building toward that you've been stuck on for some time. This could be something from your vision board that seems out of reach, a business goal that's been eluding your team, or a dream your family has together.

Make the End the Beginning: Often, the problem can be resolved if we stop thinking about what the next step should be, and think instead of what the next-to-last step should be. On a long sheet of butcher paper or whiteboard, write the end goal at the far right.

Walk It Back: Now, instead of thinking about your *first* step, think about the *last* step you would take before reaching that goal. Then think about what step would be necessary right before that. Continue the process until you've arrived at a step you can complete immediately – then go do that right now!

Why It Works: Much as we discussed in the chapter on the importance of making decisions, sometimes when a goal seems very far away, the sheer number of intermediary steps necessary becomes overwhelming. This process forces you to think about those steps as small, concrete action items, with the added benefit that when you're done, you have an immediate task to complete – and checking that task off creates motion, so the next task will benefit from that positive inertia!

EXERCISE **Exercise Get in Alignment**

Objective: To ensure that your organization's goals are in sync with your core beliefs and ultimate vision.

INSTRUCTIONS

Focus on the Hardest Parts: Any business has a list of projects, goals, or dreams that have proven frustrating, if not impossible, to implement. Whatever that list is for your group, get them all on the board where everyone can see them.

Find Their Fit: Now, take your list of core business values or principles – every business has one somewhere – and match each problem on the board to the value or principle it aligns with.

What's Out of Place? You're likely to find that some of the problems you've been stuck on don't actually align all that well with the core values of your organization. This doesn't mean that it has to be thrown out! It just means the group should discuss how to reframe the problem so that it comes into alignment. Often, people allow problems to remain unresolved because they feel subconsciously that solving them doesn't actually matter all that much. Forcing each current issue into a box with a core business value will create a clear link between *what the problem is* and *why we need to solve it*.

Transform and Succeed

EXERCISE 1

Exercise The Benjamin Franklin Approach to New Habits

Objective: To replace a group of undesirable habits with actions that better serve your goals.

INSTRUCTIONS

Choose Your Virtues: Benjamin Franklin's autobiography discusses his personal development plan, which aligns quite well with what we now know scientifically about habit formation. Franklin selected 13 virtues that he saw as essential to a good life; for him, these were things like "temperance," "order," and "industry." You're not Benjamin Franklin, so your list is likely to be different. What you're looking for is a category where you feel you're missing the mark on a specific habit. For example, if your goal is to cut wasteful spending, you might choose "financial discipline." Though Franklin used 13 virtues, I recommend selecting 12, so that it's logical to spend one month on each of them, then repeat the process each year.

Add Your Actions: For each virtue, write one short sentence that explains your goal using active verbs. For example, Franklin's sentence on "temperance" was "eat not to dullness; drink not to elevation." Each month, place that month's virtue and action sentence somewhere that you'll see it constantly.

Turn Habits into Data: Franklin did this step by creating a paper calendar that he reviewed each day, making a mark in the column for any day when he felt he'd failed in his goal. Today, there are a host of options from paper to digital apps; whichever suits you best, the key is to adopt a system that enables you to capture an ongoing picture of your progress.

Rotate and Repeat: You now have a set of 12 life virtues, with 12 corresponding action sentences. Each month, focus on one, collect data, and think intentionally about it each night. At the same time each year, review progress, consider tweaking your 12 virtues or 12 sentences, and repeat.

Stumbling Blocks and Strategies to Overcome Them

1. Actions and Beliefs Out of Sync

Stumbling Block: The simple fact is that most people don't think that hard about consistency between their actions and beliefs. In fact, simply reading this book means you're likely to have already thought about this concept far more than the average person does in their lifetime. Because of this, one source of friction is often the intersection between people who are dedicated to aligning actions with beliefs and people for whom that isn't a prominent consideration.

Strategy to Overcome: When you find yourself dealing with a person or group whose actions seem out of sync with their professed values, it's helpful to frame the situation as confusion rather than conflict. Even nonreligious people react to charges of hypocrisy more strongly than almost anything else, so pointing

Transform and Succeed

it out directly as an accusation is unlikely to work. Instead, present it as your own confusion: "I might be missing something here, but it seems like blind-copying managers on emails to coworkers is out of line with our commitment to total honesty within the group. Can you help me understand what I got wrong?"

2. Settling for "Trying"

Stumbling Block: We each have an inner critic that we're constantly trying to assuage; sometimes, when we're not seeing the results we desire, we allow ourselves the "out" of telling him: "Oh well – at least I tried." This compromise lets us feel better about ourselves and quiets the inner critic, even though nothing material about the situation has changed. When this becomes a habit, we stagnate and growth stops in whatever arena we allow it.

Strategy to Overcome: The key is to develop a quick, simple way to confront yourself with the reality that trying isn't good enough. Your *intent* doesn't matter all that much; your *results* matter immensely. To accomplish this, simply tweak the sentence. Whenever you hear your inner voice saying, "At least I tried," add this new ending: ". . . but trying isn't doing. What else can I try?"

This is helpful whether you're talking to your own inner critic or talking to a teammate or employee with a habit of letting themselves off the hook. Just change "What else can I try?" to "What else can *we* try?"

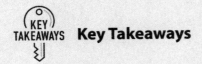

In this chapter, we discussed ways to transform dreams into reality. Though individual methods might vary from person to person and across different contexts, there's one eternal truth at the heart of it all: Intention doesn't change anything until it's attached to an *action*. This is crucial because we know that motion begets more motion, making each new step in the process just a bit easier.

As you transform an intangible dream into a reality you can touch, you'll learn to use each success as a launching point for further development, never growing complacent, always striving forward to reach things that seemed out of reach just a short time ago. And though you're certain to hit unforeseen glitches, those first small actions in the direction of your goal will give you the persistence and consistency to overcome, always moving forward to the vision you began in the first chapter.

Chapter 5

Personal SHIFTS (Values)

Personal Shifts Through Values

On your leadership journey, personal values serve as a compass that can guide decisions, influence behaviors, and shape the culture within organizations. Recent global events, such as the pandemic, have highlighted how pivotal these values are, not only in our personal lives but also in the realms of leadership and team dynamics. As leaders, even small shifts in our values can create ripple effects, having an impact on the way we lead, the environment we foster, and the outcomes we achieve.

This chapter delves into the critical role that personal values play in driving leadership shifts and influencing team dynamics. By understanding and prioritizing core values, leaders can navigate challenges with integrity and purpose, fostering a culture that aligns with both personal convictions and organizational goals.

We will explore two key lessons in this chapter:

- **Understanding the core values that drive personal leadership:** Discover how your fundamental values influence your leadership style and decision-making processes, and how these values can either strengthen or weaken your leadership effectiveness.

- **How values affect team performance and organizational culture:** Learn how the values you uphold as a leader trickle down to your team, shaping the overall performance and the cultural fabric of your organization.

By the end of this chapter, you will not only have a deeper understanding of your own values but also practical strategies to align these values with your leadership approach, driving both personal and organizational growth.

Of Course, Values Change

We like to say that our values don't change, but that's an awfully broad statement that doesn't bear much scrutiny. Certainly, there are some things we would never budge on – principles we hold dear enough to risk everything for. However, history shows that those sorts of values are actually pretty small in number.

Many things we considered important at one time or another fell far down the list of priorities in the recent global pandemic. Most people's focus narrowed like a laser beam on one thing: remaining alive and healthy. This priority moved to the top of the pile, and understandably so. Some put family vacations on the back burner, relocated their family, or made other major adjustments like working from home in an effort to navigate unprecedented circumstances. Perhaps you did this as well. When we create SHIFTS in our values as leaders, those SHIFTS create additional SHIFTS in our relationships, careers, organizations, and communities.

One of the greatest indicators of value SHIFTS during the pandemic was what the media termed the Great Resignation. Kim Parker and Juliana Menasce Horowitz reported in an article for the Pew Research Center that one of the major reasons so many people quit their jobs between 2021 and 2022 was because they felt disrespected at work.[1] Of course, several other reasons were cited. I think the pandemic revealed the true values of many leaders as they made decisions in an environment fraught with uncertainty. It's just like the strength of a foundation is tested during a storm. People's strength was tested. The human spirit was tested. If a leader valued people over tasks and accomplishments, the pandemic revealed it. However, if a leader valued profits and control, taking advantage of the disenfranchised, or winning an election over human life, the pandemic also revealed it. If a person had not paid enough attention to their health, relationships, or financial plans, the pandemic revealed it. This difficult time turned a bright spotlight on how imperative it is for leaders to guide and love those around them, helping them to clarify an inclusive vision for the future. When we do this, we create value SHIFTS for others and ourselves.

APPLICATION

Take a Seat and Choose Your Values

When our church moved into a new building, we faced a seemingly simple decision: choosing chairs for our members and pastors. As we discussed different options, someone made an observation that completely shifted the direction of our conversation – and our thinking.

This individual pointed out that while we were considering more comfortable chairs for the pastors, the ones selected for our congregation were less so. He raised a crucial question: If we were genuinely committed to promoting the idea that our members are equal in worth to our leaders – a challenging message to convey in our cultural context – shouldn't we

101

ensure that everyone, leaders and members alike, sits in the same quality chairs? His point was undeniable. The leadership team unanimously agreed. As leaders, our actions needed to reflect the values we preached each week. I remarked that there is no difference in the physical needs of a leader and a member. If our values don't translate into our decisions, behaviors, and actions, they are meaningless.

How Our Values Were Recognized

At that time, we could only afford basic plastic chairs, so we ensured that everyone had the same seating, regardless of status. Later, as our resources grew, we upgraded to higher quality, more comfortable chairs – but not until we could do so for *everyone*. Over time, this decision became a powerful symbol of our values. Many leaders from various organizations and faith communities who attended our events took notice. They remarked on how this simple, consistent choice resonated with them, reinforcing our message of equality and shared respect.

I'm not suggesting that every organization must follow this exact practice. Every group must determine the values that align with its own mission and objectives. However, this experience illustrates how we can create SHIFTS in our organizations by consistently aligning what people See and Hear with our core values, as discussed in our six-step approach to transforming leadership mindsets.

Cultures Are Built on Doing the Right Thing, Because It's the Right Thing to Do

There was a time when purchasing organic food was difficult because organic foods were not available everywhere. That has changed dramatically, especially with the emergence of Texas-based Whole Foods Market, which changed the landscape of grocery shopping for millions by connecting communities with organic farmers, farm-to-table foods, gourmet foods, and more. Whole Foods, now owned by Amazon, has also become more affordable because of the merger. The company proudly shares its values, transparency regarding leaders' salaries, and its emphasis on diversity and inclusion. One of their core values even assumes they have an obligation to include healthcare benefits and gym memberships that can provide their employees with a healthier lifestyle. These perks align with their values. Do your perks align with your organization's values? When they do, success is often the result.

Values Are Leadership Currency That SHIFTS Integrity and Trust

Dr. David Oyedepo once said to me, "If you don't have values, you don't have value." This struck me hard. When you define your values and then live by those values, you resist the temptations to make a quick dollar in a crooked way, which may provide material value up-front, but in the long term costs you respect, trust, and integrity. I like to tell my team that their integrity is their currency. For example, if I needed a loan right now, there are people I would reach out to for assistance. These people trust me because I have never misled them or lied to them. My values have led me in a way that has been consistently visible to those around me. You'll always be respected for living authentically. You'll gain leadership currency, which is like having cash in the bank – or, as leadership author John Maxwell puts it, "change in your pocket."[2]

People do not have to mimic your values in their own lives, follow them perfectly in the workplace, or even agree with your values or the decisions they lead you to make. Regardless of how it's perceived, leaders make tough decisions and initiate difficult conversations in line with their core values. When you model this consistently, others will respect your boundaries and know that you are not a yes person. In the organizations I lead, I always try my best to model the values I'd like to see in others. Nothing erodes our credibility like hypocrisy or lying. Accountability is key.

For example, in one of my organizations people find it surprising that I have made myself accountable to the board of directors. At the management level, my team and I make hard decisions together as we prepare budgets and set goals for the year ahead. We demonstrate what we do with transparency. I present my ideas to the board and then I abide by whatever they decide. The benefits are immeasurable. My experience is that this gives everyone a sense of safety and it earns me respect from others. It also provides empowerment. And I believe that empowering others translates into income and successful succession planning, as well. When a business truly empowers its people to make decisions, both on the spot and otherwise, it speaks volumes for the mindset of its leaders. SHIFTS take place. There is action. There is valuation.

APPLICATION

Values in Action

Values SHIFTS are active processes. In 2021 my organization conducted a worldwide study and assessment of both aspiring and current leadership. We did this so that we could SHIFT. We wanted to provide the best leadership materials and training going forward. We yearned to produce specific training that would shift mindsets and speak to the needs of the people. Our survey measured both quantitative and qualitative responses. It took several months to execute and compile the results, but the guidelines that emerged were invaluable. As responses to our online questionnaire rolled in over the months, we clearly saw a common denominator of leadership values in action. Thousands wanted to build their own entrepreneurial experience or rise to a certain level of leadership standards. Everything kept pointing back to the importance of maintaining values and shifting mindsets for new generations to enhance those values. It was awe inspiring. We grabbed on to that and rode the wave.

APPLICATION

Values with Purpose

We soon realized that our international survey not only provided inside information to our team, sparking ideas of new and advanced programs we could offer, but it also organically provided a unique forum for meaningful discussions. Conversations were sparked among our leadership team, our employees, our church members, and those who attended our seminars and conferences. The results were straightforward and revealing. This inventory told us that when people learn how to apply tools and techniques to make SHIFTS, they can more easily align their behaviors with the organization's values, desired outcomes, and ultimate goals. They became *values* in *action* with *purpose*. That was huge.

When we administered the questionnaire on several continents, including North America, Africa, Asia, and Europe, participants let us know the traits, values, and characteristics they wanted in leadership. This helped my organizations greatly because we could provide SHIFTS to our followers and give them meaningful goals to aim for. Here are some of the most popular responses we received regarding character and its essence in a leadership role.

Honesty

Integrity

Inspiring

Empathetic

Understanding

Knowledgeable

Reliable

Forward-thinking

Visionary

Creative

Passionate

Kind

Intuitive

Respectful

Entrepreneurial

Caring

Goal-oriented

Easy to work with (cooperative)

Credible

The importance of credibility, specifically, helped us to lean toward our respondents in a tangible way. We understood that when participants perceived credibility in their leadership, along with an honest, straightforward approach to sharing information, they felt a sense of pride and a stakeholdership. The sense of team spirit carried over. When the respondent's personal values aligned with organizational values, people felt a sense of ownership and commitment. These are powerful traits. Shifting these important values forward and upward is what grows people and their companies. Minds expand when mind SHIFTS expand.

Values Are Transparent

As leaders, it's our job to provide products, services, and opportunities people can believe in, get behind, and be proud of. Our values must be as transparent as these offerings. Share your values and your business model with employees and use it to attract new, top talent. Values aren't meant to be a best-kept secret. They are meant to be shared and to inspire others. If employees are not motivated by your leadership or your vision and values, you will experience constant frustration, and so will they. Do your employees share your vision? This doesn't mean you have to agree on everything or see the future exactly the same way. Different generations will take different approaches. It's healthy at times to agree to disagree. The bottom line is that a leader genuinely respects the role of their people's positions, no matter what the level of work, so that the organization's goals and success can be appreciated and invested in. Your values should match your people's purpose. Otherwise, you will be seen as hypocritical. If leaders boast they believe that people are the organization's greatest asset, but then act in an opposite and disrespectful way toward the people, the values match is lost and will be very hard to regain.

What About Bias?

Is there some degree of bias and expectation in a making a list of values and sharing them? Yes. There's always going to be bias and expectation about the future. There's bias about agreeing to respect one another. And there's bias in commitment to do the best one can do. There is always going to be some element of pushback when it comes to values. There are people who will oppose certain values and belief systems. This is to be expected. But when there is respect and when expectations are clearly outlined, trust emerges. Civility becomes the order of the day. Trust is key.

Trust and Values

When a leader breaks their promises, they quickly erode the very trust they must lean on to lead effectively, and their credibility declines. I'd like to emphasize here that once this happens, both trust and credibility are very difficult to regain. Sam Chand, renowned international business and leadership consultant, said in his book, *Turbo Leadership*, "When you're honest with your people, your authenticity, genuineness and integrity will rise to a higher level with them, and they will know you are a truth-teller. They'll take you at your word because you'll have shown them that you see them as equals."[3]

So what do you consider to be the cornerstones of trust and reliability? Perhaps they include open communication, acknowledging trust as a mutual exchange, respect for others' differences and opinions, or simply doing what you say you're going to do. Here's a fast exercise to practice with your team. Ask the team these questions and have them share their thoughts in small groups. Responding to these scenarios will be a reliable guidepost for you as their leader.

EXERCISE **Exercise Team Values Alignment Workshop**

Objective: To facilitate a team exercise that aligns group values with the overall leadership vision, fostering a cohesive and value-driven organizational culture.

INSTRUCTIONS

Preparation: Gather your team for a dedicated workshop focused on values alignment. Provide them with a list of common organizational values such as integrity, accountability, respect, and innovation. You can also include the values identified in the first exercise.

Ask each team member to review the list and add any additional values they believe are important for the team's success.

Group Discussion: Divide the team into small groups and ask each group to discuss the following questions:

- Which values from the list resonate most with your personal beliefs and why?

- How do these values currently manifest in our team's behavior and decisions?

- Are there any values that we, as a team, need to emphasize more?

Values Prioritization: Reconvene as a full team and ask each group to share their top three values. Discuss the reasons behind their choices and how these values can contribute to the team's success.

(continued)

(continued)

As a team, prioritize a final list of three to five core values that everyone agrees should guide the team's actions and decisions moving forward.

Implementation Strategy: Ask your team the following:

- Do you believe these top three values can be taught? How will you teach them to others?

- Do you feel you need to expand or further develop these traits within yourself? If yes, what is your plan to do so?

- Develop a strategy for embedding these core values into the team's daily operations. This could include creating team norms, setting specific goals related to each value, and identifying behaviors that reflect these values.

- Assign team members to monitor and encourage adherence to these values in meetings, projects, and other team activities.

Follow-Up and Reflection: Schedule regular check-ins to evaluate how well the team is living out these values. Use these sessions to celebrate successes, address challenges, and make adjustments as needed.

Encourage open dialogue about the impact of these values on team dynamics and overall performance.

Outcome: This exercise will help your team align their personal and professional values with the overarching leadership vision, creating a more unified and value-driven organizational culture. It also fosters a sense of ownership and accountability among team members as they actively participate in defining and upholding the team's core values.

Our values are key to healthy and positive SHIFTS. Values influence changes in behavior and improvement in team performance, provided they continue to remain relevant and keep shifting forward. Yes. Values shift. The core belief system might stay the same, depending on the industry and the organization, but the values evolve and keep changing to include new talent, stronger opinions, and more innovative processes. We see this especially in multigenerational organizations.

There's only one way to shift values, and that is to shift the mindsets about them to enable transformative leadership techniques to flourish. Transformative leaders are intentional about aligning the values of their team members with the values of their organization. Behaviors that result from value SHIFTS are not accidental.

Guardians of Integrity

Think of it this way: Values can become the guardians of an organization's integrity and grit. They are critical because they define the desired behaviors of leadership via a leader's personal and professional conduct. Values are woven into the fabric of your corporate culture, which will be discussed further in Chapter 6.

> When you work and lead in an environment where there are established values, you can begin to follow your dreams and live your passion. That's when the chances of achieving balance in your professional and personal life SHIFTS forward dramatically.
>
> —Sam Adeyemi

Values Can Shift Positively or Negatively

At one time, Arthur Andersen LLP was considered one of the "Big Five" accounting and consultancy firms in the world. Its operations spread around the world, with 28,000 employees at the peak of its operations. The greater part of its later growth came from its consulting arm. Their expansion came with a shift in values. Susan Squires and her coauthors explained this shift in the book *Arthur Andersen: Shifting Values, Unexpected Consequences*. They said, "Accounting was about doing it right and following the rules. Consulting was about thinking outside the box and making the rules."[4] There was a gradual shift from the strict application of rules that govern the accounting profession to the creative innovation applied to problem-solving in consulting. This allowed for the entanglement with Enron that led to the end of both companies.

As leaders, we will always be confronted with opportunities in our quest for growth. Some will align with our organizations' values; some will not. Will we be intentional about staying true to our core values and shifting minds to align with them, or will we allow our values to be compromised in search of a fast buck?

There are countless news stories about companies and their leaders who are caught in criminal activities. Each time I see one, it stops me in my tracks, thinking, "How could this have happened? What were they thinking? What a shame all these employees will lose their jobs." This is what I meant when I stated that as leaders, we are the guardians of our organization's integrity. When one part of an organization pursues a course of action that abuses the community's values, someone always knows something is going on. But if the values haven't been ingrained in them properly, they might say nothing until it's too late. This is why I never underestimate the importance of helping everyone I can to shift their mindset to a higher level of values-driven opportunities and often greater prosperity whenever possible.

Leaders Shape Values

In my book, *Dear Leader: Your Flagship Guide to Successful Leadership,* I share various ways a leader can use their influence to shape the values of their teams or organizations. Here are a few:

- Create a blueprint and define your personal values.
- Be sure your values align with the values you set for your organization.
- Create and build a list of core values. Make this your cultural blueprint for moving forward and achieving success.
- Continue to model your organization's values.
- Let core values attract top talent to your organization.
- Reward behavior publicly; correct and redirect behavior privately.

Love as a Fundamental Value

I called one of our staff members into my office, drew attention to his misconduct, and handed him his sack letter (in Great Britain this is a term used to fire someone or ask them to leave). I simply pointed out that the decision was based on our policies, which he had violated, and assured him of my love and willingness to help him get another job. I share this story because I am sometimes asked if showing team members or employees love in a business environment would not make everyone lax with the rules. On the contrary, love at its highest level, which is self-sacrificing, is the best way to motivate humans. It also motivates us to apply correction when necessary and to provoke improvement in the ones we love and lead. The gentleman in my story would go on to become one of the most committed volunteers in our organization.

In their book, *Love As a Business Strategy: Resilience, Belonging and Success,* Anwar et al. discuss how shifting from a culture of greed to a culture of love resulted in a turnaround for their organization. They assert, "How we treat each other creates or destroys culture."[5] The authors were able to create an environment that fosters innovation, efficiency, and high-performing teams by shaping behaviors with inclusion, empathy, vulnerability, trust, empowerment, and forgiveness, which they call the *six pillars of love*.

Love Is the Recognition and Celebration of Value in Others

I see love as the recognition and celebration of value in others. Seeing human beings as the most valuable assets on our planet influences our attitude toward people in profound ways. It helps us to cherish others and to care about them. It also helps us to spot gaps in their lives. It is beneath human dignity to go without food or to lack clothing and protection from the elements. This motivates us to give and serve. It also motivates us to forgive, which requires writing off emotional debts. This reminds me of the description by Stephen R. Covey in *The 7 Habits of Highly Effective People* when he says we have emotional bank accounts with one another in our relationships.[6] With acts of love and kindness, we make deposits. When we offend or apply discipline, we are making withdrawals. We can make withdrawals without destroying relationships if we have been making deposits all along through acts of love. But making withdrawals without having made deposits puts the account in the red and destroys relationships. Teams where members make a lot of deposits are able to communicate and act without fear. They resolve issues easily and are high performing. Is it any surprise that when Jesus Christ was asked, "Which is the greatest commandment?" He answered, "Love."[7]

Carrying Values Forward Through Succession Planning

People often ask me, "How do you plan to carry your organization's values forward?" That is an excellent question. None of us will remain in the same position forever. In the SHIFTS model, the letter T stand for Transform. It says, "Your decisions transform your actions for making those big bold moves!" But who sets the tone? This question is crucial, because the tone will always outlive the tone-setter.

High-Profile Organizations Who Set the Tone

I have a friend who is a speaker and trainer. She's worked with hundreds of notable individuals and prestigious clients throughout the world. She's interviewed political dignitaries like Henry Kissinger and best-selling authors like Stephen Covey. She's benchmarked hundreds of companies on their leadership styles and learning and development programs. We recently chatted and she told me about two impressive organizations she interviewed for a special project a while back, and both examples really stuck with me.

One was The Bank of Montreal, now known as BMO in North America – a multinational bank and financial investment company based in Toronto. About 15 years ago they created what they called a Possibilities Center. My friend shared with me that she felt the name of the department alone summed up how the bank approached growing and developing its people to reach their full potential. They were one of the first financial institutions to make such a bold move in employee training, and their success in these efforts made them a benchmark for other financial institutions in the years ahead. The apparent purpose and focus of the center at that time was to prepare employees for succession roles ahead of time, ensuring a steady pipeline of leaders steeped in the company's values and vision. Good idea.

Another example she shared was about the importance of being ready, when the time comes, to pass the baton. This trip had led her to travel to many Ritz Carlton Hotel locations where she interviewed everyone, from managers and administrators down to bellhops, bartenders, and heads of housekeeping. She learned that the Ritz Carlton hotels (now Marriott) charged each new hire that on their first day on the job to already begin looking for and training their own replacement, a strategy written about in the book *The New Gold Standard* by Joseph A. Michelli.[7] This attitude has carried forward into many businesses today. The decision to take a position also requires the responsibility of seeking out your replacement. The insecure need not apply; it takes gusto to follow through on this. However, it may, indeed, be the only way to make positive employee promotions and SHIFTS going forward. For one thing, it enables you to prepare for advancement and it organically trains and prepares others for constantly shifting up and forward. It's a win-win for everyone and helps eliminate any room for insecurity or possessiveness in an organization or leadership role.

Core Values Matter

Core values are the foundation on which your culture will thrive. I will get into specific culture SHIFTS in the next chapter, which can be mind-blowing. But for now, when it comes to values, be the example. Do the right thing because it's the right thing to do. Ask yourself, "Does this action make sense in light of the values we've created and abide by in our organization?" If the answer is yes then you've got a green light.

A simple lesson when it comes to values SHIFTS is to always remember that when you take care of the inside, the outside will take care of itself. Your company, its culture, and your ultimate success will always reflect the values you hold near and dear.

> Core values help us to create a stronger framework that allows us to evaluate and shift toward better choices as leaders.
>
> —Sam Adeyemi

Abiding by your values is a daily choice. Choose to energize others, not drain them. Values and establishing a high morale go together. So always lead by example. Mirror the behavior you want to see in others. Be trustworthy and establish your honest intentions verbally. Communicate clearly. Establish clear expectations. Remain humble even when you're at the top – or perhaps I should say, *especially* when you've reached the top. Radiate a positive attitude and demeanor whenever possible. And approach your work with creativity. Creative energy makes the difference between getting the job done and getting it done with distinction.

Just like your GPS plots the course you'll take when you travel, your values will be your guide for your inner thoughts and behavior toward others. Your core values will never let you down. They will steer you toward every situation in life. They will give you peace of mind that you are doing the right thing at the right time given the choices available. Values are the heart of your personal authenticity. I have tried to convey this strongly with my teams and in my prior books. I try to use my values as a guide for all of my decisions. I might not always get it right, but using them consistently SHIFTS me forward. I promise it will do the same for you. It's also a gateway to your development and the growth of your organization's culture. This is where the rubber meets the road, as far as I am concerned. We build a strong culture when we remain vigilant and aware of the patterns emerging around us. Life and learning are constant struggle, but we can find harmony in strong values, internal inspiration, and a culture that will lead us to shift forward like never before. Culture SHIFTS can be a flagship to the growth and success you are seeking. How do I know this? I know that when we better understand our core values, as we've done in this chapter, we can build a stronger framework for our people. When we validate our approach to doing this, we start making wiser, better choices overall. The new, smarter choices we make, ultimately, decide our future. The point here, as I mentioned previously, is that the past does not predict outcomes. New choices and new SHIFTS will decide where you are headed. And that is here and now.

If values-led leadership has taught us anything, it is that organizations do not have to sacrifice social consciousness on the altar of maximum profits and employee performance. Yes, values do translate into a healthy, profitable bottom line. My organizations experience this transfer daily. Consumers used to buy products and services despite how they felt about the organizations that sold them. That attitude has shifted greatly.

Today, values-led organizations appeal to buyers. The late actor Paul Newman started a food company focusing on salad dressings and other foods. His company, to this day, gives every penny of profit from his Newman's Own food line to children's charities. Stores like Target and Ben & Jerry's Ice Cream do social audits and contribute to communities nationwide. These intentional actions gain more loyal customers and greater sales for both retailers. Polls show continuously that the most successful organizations and their leaders place enormous emphasis on company values. Included in this group are companies like McDonald's, the South Carolina Police Department, Patagonia, Whole Foods Market, Odwalla, Disney, Virgin Group, Ltd., and the Chicago Bears. Many go so far as to publish statements in their annual reports on their commitment to social responsibility.

Exercise Personal Values Assessment and Prioritization

EXERCISE 1

Objective: To help readers identify, assess, and prioritize their personal and professional values, ensuring alignment with their leadership roles and organizational culture.

INSTRUCTIONS

Self-Reflection: Begin by listing at least 10 values that you believe are important in both your personal and professional life. Examples include integrity, honesty, empathy, innovation, and teamwork.

Reflect on recent decisions you've made in your leadership role. Which of these values were most influential in those

(continued)

(continued)

decisions? Were there any values you neglected that might have led to different outcomes?

Values Ranking: Rank your list of values from most to least important. Consider how each value influences your behavior, decision-making, and interactions with others.

Identify your top three values. These should be the guiding principles that consistently shape your leadership actions and decisions.

Alignment with Leadership Role: For each of your top three values, write a brief paragraph explaining how it aligns with your current leadership role and how it influences your team and organizational culture.

Reflect on any discrepancies between your personal values and the values promoted within your organization. How do these discrepancies affect your effectiveness as a leader?

Action Plan: Develop an action plan to better integrate your top three values into your daily leadership practices. This might include setting specific goals, such as improving transparency in communication (if honesty is a top value) or fostering a more collaborative environment (if teamwork is a priority).

Set a timeline for implementing these changes and identify any potential obstacles that could hinder your progress.

Outcome: This exercise will help you gain clarity on your core values, understand their impact on your leadership, and create a practical plan for aligning your actions with these values to enhance your leadership effectiveness.

STUMBLING
BLOCKS

Stumbling Block and Strategies to Overcome It

1. Aligning Personal and Organizational Values

Stumbling Block: Any organization of sufficient size will inevitably have members whose values aren't perfectly aligned, and that's a good thing. We already have a word for a large group of people who believe perfectly identical things: we call those cults, and I doubt you'd like to see much similarity between your organization and a mindless cult, which definitionally stifles innovation and new ideas. This means your values have to be specific enough to be of value to your group, but not so granular that people of widely varying worldviews and belief systems can't all fit within them. So how do you find the sweet spot?

Strategy to Overcome: Be intentional in talking about the importance of sensitivity to others' culture and belief systems. Values vary when applied to different parts of an organization's culture or different locations in the world. Ask for insights and don't ignore other possibilities to executive values and caring.

- **Hammer the Point:** Don't just visit the subject of values occasionally. Take time to discuss in group meetings and get input from others. Your group's values must be simple and constant enough that each employee can recall them with ease and align their decision with in every situation they'll encounter.

- **Display Them from the Top Down:** Remind employees of the enormous value of values by verbally connecting your own decisions to them in group meetings. Some leaders even discuss values in the context of a return on integrity (another form of return on investment).

People do what they see their leaders doing. Be aware of your behavior on and off the job.

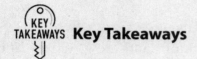

Key Takeaways

At the core of leadership lies a set of values that reflect how people view themselves and the world around them. Values are not wishy-washy; they are constant, providing a stable foundation for decision-making and guiding how we choose to spend our time and resources. The values we embody as leaders touch not just the minds but also the hearts of those we lead. When these values are aligned with actions, they foster trust, authenticity, and a sense of shared purpose, which in turn drives optimal performance within teams and organizations.

As we've explored in this chapter, value-driven leadership is about creating alignment between personal beliefs and team dynamics, resulting in a culture that thrives on mutual respect and integrity. Values shape our leadership, influence team performance, and define the culture we build.

In Chapter 6, we will dive deeper into the importance of culture and how to build one of greatness. Specifically, we'll explore professional SHIFTS, focusing on navigating the challenges of working with multigenerational teams and leading from a distance. You'll discover how the SHIFTS model can be applied to foster collaboration, innovation, and success across diverse and geographically dispersed teams.

Chapter 6

Professional SHIFTS (Team, Multigenerational, Distance)

Leading Across Generations and Distance: Redefining Team Success

In Chapter 5, we discussed shifting our personal values. But there are many kinds of people, varying in age, ethnicity, background, and more. This chapter discusses how to take those personal shifts and weave them together across your team, the many generations and cultures it includes, and even the workers who don't report physically to the office – because no matter how much shifting each employee does personally, if those shifts don't all gel into one coherent organizational shift, people will waste time pulling in multiple directions.

Creating Culture SHIFTS in Your Organization

As a leader, you are the architect of the culture you hope to build within your team or organization and the SHIFTS you wish to see happen. Everything starts with the leaders in the organization. When it comes to culture, your organization will reflect on the outside precisely the values that its embraces on the inside. That's when leaders transition to become situational heroes for the good of the people. A situational hero is someone

125

who rises to the occasion and enhances the organization's culture with their behavior, which we'll discuss later in the chapter.

Culture SHIFTS are powerful. They can greatly increase an organization's worth and profitability – some say more than 50%. I believe it to be even higher. SHIFTS can improve global presence and perceived value. Teach your leaders to see the importance of intentional organizational culture and the significant role each person plays within it. Culture combined with talent or human capital is a force of nature made up of behaviors, attitudes, values, personalities, environments, rites and rituals, and storytelling.

Workers look for security and consistency in their cultural environment. It's human nature that people don't respond well to chaos, unpredictable times, threatening situations, or severe changes all at once. This is where culture is so important. If employees feel surrounded by a dependable and stabilizing force, when things start to shift, they automatically become more confident and open-minded to handle the SHIFTS ahead. This is one of the reasons why my own organization survived the most notable worldwide pandemic of all time.

Culture Creates Stability

Like most families, our family stayed together during the lockdowns stemming from the COVID-19 pandemic. We were in the United States. However, when it was time to resume our pre-COVID routine of moving between the United States and Nigeria, my wife and I developed strong intuition. That intuition said to stay in the United States. Intuition is critical to leadership because it helps us to navigate uncertainty and assess risks. Rational thinking alone might not be adequate to manage situations with high levels of uncertainty and unpredictability.

Leadership expert John Maxwell lists "the law of intuition" as the eighth law in his book, *The 21 Irrefutable Laws of Leadership*.[1] He describes intuition as the ability to "smell things" and to read a situation before we have all the facts. We went with our intuition and were away from our church in Nigeria for about three years. That phase has since ended, but I now meet leaders around the world who ask what we did that made most of our operations run seamlessly without the organization falling apart. The secret is in the culture that we have built intentionally through training programs, including the Daystar Academy, Daystar Leadership Academy, Daystar Business Academy, and the Daystar Skill Acquisition Program. We also celebrate training events like the Excellence in Leadership Conference and the Strategic Leadership Congress. Our core values, which form the acronym I.R.E.A.L. (which stands for Innovation, Righteousness, Excellence, Accountability, and Love), also play a major role in shaping our culture. Thankfully, we had spent years intentionally using these events and processes to shape the culture of each organization in our charge so the mental and emotional infrastructure was already there when we needed it. Our existing structures and systems play a major role in shaping the way we respond to situations. It's part of our culture to shift the weight of leadership responsibility to people on a mass scale, enabling our systems to run even in the absence of our top leaders. Not only were we – the two most senior leaders – away for a long period, our COO, the third in the leadership chain, also left for higher pursuits with our blessings – yet our operations continued to run effectively. What happened could be called an organizational miracle, in our view. And things organically, as they do in life, moved forward.

Professional SHIFTS (Team, Multigenerational, Distance)

Creating a Culture of Service Excellence

One of my organizations hosted a retreat for C-level leaders at The Oberoi in Marrakech, Morocco. My global manager, David Ayodele, arrived ahead of all our team members and the participants. Then he received a little surprise from The Oberoi's culture of service excellence. He was attending a meeting with staff from the hotel when housekeeping cleaned his room. He returned to see that they had replaced his toothpaste with a new toothpaste of the same brand. They also left a typewritten note saying: "Dear Mr. Ayodele, we hope you are doing well. We observed that your toothpaste is about finished, and we took the opportunity to place a new one for your convenience. Kindly let us know if there is anything we can improve during your stay. Warm regards, Your Housekeeper." David was blown away by this display of care. They even took time to type and print the note!

I shared this experience with one of our clients. He mentioned that The Oberoi's culture of service excellence is used in a case study for a management program he attended at Harvard Business School.[2] This shows that The Oberoi's culture of service excellence is not accidental. It is intentional and consistent across all their locations. Stan Toler and Alan Nelson awakened me to the culture of service excellence several years ago when I read their book, *The Five Star Church*.[3] The authors applied the principles used in the hospitality industry to church ministry. It was a paradigm shift for me. I shared the principles with all our staff at our weekly meetings and we began using them immediately. The principles that we applied with results form part of the curriculum for the course "Building an Excellence-Oriented Organization" at our Daystar Leadership Academy to this day.

Cultural Migration

I heard the story of a family who came to Nigeria from the United States. The parents had been before, but their children were visiting for the first time. One evening, one of the children cried out, "Mum, Mum, help me. I'm going blind." The mum panicked at first and then realized what had happened. The child was not going blind. There was a power outage, which is a regular occurrence in Nigeria. But this child had never experienced one. Her immediate interpretation of the situation was that she was blind.

This story illustrates how what is considered to be normal is different for people in different places. A leader needs to define what is normal or acceptable for their group by creating SHIFTS in people's mindsets. This will allow for a fairly uniform interpretation of situations.

For example, you might aspire to create a culture of excellence in an environment where mediocrity is normal lifestyle. Perhaps there is low value for cleanliness and aesthetics in the community. Your organization members will be cultural migrants moving between the culture in your organization and the prevailing culture in the community. You will need to reinforce the prevailing mindset in your organization in every possible way. But the place to start is to know where your people are coming from in terms of mindsets, beliefs, and values. Perhaps, the previous story indicates why many leadership strategies and practices brought in from Western countries don't necessarily always work in developing economies. The teachers of these principles have never experienced what is considered the norm, or what's acceptable for people in developing economies.

I later described the issue of power outages to a chauffeur in the United Kingdom and he said he had not personally experienced a power outage in 20 years. To create SHIFTS in culture, you must know what is the existing "normal" for the team, organization, or community you seek to lead. Then you must paint a clear picture of the "new normal" and how your group will go about achieving it. Paint a vision of the possibilities.

Revisit the SHIFTS model in this book. Culture really focuses on the word *Succeed* in the model. Your actions lead to success and your actions are a huge part of your organization's culture.

You can feel and experience an organization's culture the minute you step into its space. It can be an office, a church, an arena, a ship, a banking facility, a hospital, and many other environments. Culture is not just about a mission statement or vision statement hanging on the wall in the entryway. It's much more. It's energy. It's human kindness. It's love. And it might indeed become the future.

What Love Has to Do with It

Are you building a culture of love? This has nothing to do with romance. I think of love as a verb: actively caring for other human beings. The intrinsic care for others is why love works at work. It means putting the people's needs ahead of your own. People know and sense when they are authentically loved and cared for. There's a ripple effect. Profits are important but humanity is absolutely critical. When we have a loving culture, profits can soar, organizations can transcend almost anything, people leave greed behind and help their fellow brother and sister. When you build a culture of love, you help establish trust and accountability, along with measurable and positive outcomes. A loving culture fosters inclusion, not exclusion. And it never sweeps problems away. It addresses them head on but with compassion and empathy. Confrontation is not a bad thing. It is not fighting. It is simply confronting the other party to find agreement and unity.

Remember how important it is when using the SHIFTS process to first See and Hear to take in what is around you to your heart center. Are people around you saying, "You make me feel worth your time. My work environment makes me feel valued, happy, and welcome each day."

Healthy, Wealthy, and Wise

According to a survey from the National Bureau of Economic Research, 85% of CEOs and CFOs believe that an unhealthy and unwell culture of workers leads to possible unethical behavior, as well as lower productivity.[4] In addition, that same survey found that 9 out of 10 leaders also believe that an improved company culture can lead to their business's increased value and better performance overall.

Employees worldwide look to be a part of cultures that encourage good health, life balance, and total wellness. Burnout cultures are yesterday's news. Working without healthy practices can lead to unhealthy employees and even unhealthy families of employees. The employee brings home the stress of an unhealthy workplace, further widening the ripple. There are lots of things an organization can do to promote a healthier culture, improve well-being, and provide a reasonable life balance and equilibrium for its workers and their families. Open those windows. Let the light and fresh air in wherever possible and it will organically nourish people's ideas, spirits, and bodies. Fresh plants and greenery make for a healthier workspace, too.

Provide incentives for achieving healthier lifestyles, like free gym memberships for employees and their families. Offer yoga classes, Pilates, or guided meditation before or after work.

Bring in a health coach regularly to speak and motivate workers. Organize walks and runs for all departments. Give people incentives to attend workshops for healthier lifestyles. Offer free magazine subscriptions and books to guide people to healthy living, cooking, and eating. Extend lunch hours to enable employees time for a brisk walk outside or to sit peacefully in a quiet zone or in the sun. Wearables to track steps are popular and might make a valued employee gift. However, do not make anything regarding better health a requirement or mandatory. Leaders are not doctors. Allow people to pace themselves and to select the type of healthy living ideas that work for them individually. Every person approaches their well-being in their own way or in their comfort zone. Some people enjoy the solitude of health practices where they are not feeling competitive or judged by others. It all starts with movement and momentum. The degree to which the person chooses to move and make lifestyle changes is personal and should always be respected. Being healthy, wealthy, and wise starts with the SHIFTS we make in our own heads first.

What has this simple culture evaluation revealed to you? How will you use this information going forward? Some organizations create culture councils, allowing people to volunteer to build the environment they'd like to work in. Ask for volunteers and then have those people shift out of those positions after one year to encourage others to get involved in contributing fun and interesting ideas. If you have any type of suggestion box in your workplace there are two keys to getting people to offer ideas. Keep suggestions private and let people know that their input is going to be read, considered, and responded to, whether or not they can be applied immediately. Thank employees for sharing ideas and for understanding there is a time, place, and budget for initiation and change.

When suggestion boxes fail, it's almost always because people are discouraged, thinking no one seems to care or take time to consider their opinions. If people take time to offer an opinion, it's your job as a leader to at least consider it and take time to read what your people are expressing.

Next, here are a few strategic practices that might help you to make your own cultural SHIFTS. If you want to help your current leaders and aspiring leaders to work more efficiently and productively, they will need a road map of strategies. Applying these strategic SHIFTS and tactics will help leaders galvanize their own leadership personalities to the personality or culture of the organization itself. Give them a try.

Strategy 1: Design a workplace around the kind of talent you want to attract and keep.

If the talent pool is in their 20s to 30s, what things can you include in the cultural feel to keep them excited and engaged? If teams are seasoned and over 50 years of age, what mind SHIFTS can you offer based on their experience and curiosity? When you create a culture around the people who make up the culture, you are helping to ensure your company's ongoing success and level of productivity and performance. You have more control than you think. We'll get into more of this later in this chapter.

Strategy 2: Be an influencer. Culture is said to be the personality of a company, just like a person has their own personality. You can't necessarily change someone's personality, but you can influence their behavior on the job by how you lead and apply the SHIFTS we've discussed. It's the same at home. If you have a 16-year-old child, you're not going to change their personality, but you can influence their behavior and decision-making going forward with your behaviors and decision-making examples. All eyes are on you as the leader. Be the example.

Strategy 3: Train and lead with calmness. No one listens to a hysterical leader. Remain calm. Remember, you set the tone. It can be confusing and challenging dealing with all types of people and relationships at the same time. We have relationships with our partners at home, our coworkers, and our family and friends. We have relationships with ourselves. What is your deeper purpose and how will you follow your North Star? Then there is the relationship we have with life itself and how we decide to lead day-by-day. Life and work can happen at breakneck speed. It's how you handle things and respond that counts most. Like I said, you set the tone. One calibrator that can help you find your center is to simply raise your standards on all these areas of life and relationships I've listed here. It doesn't have to be monumental. But when you make simple or big SHIFTS forward and upward you are automatically setting higher standards for acceptable behavior and performance. I know a teacher who adopted a simple rule years ago: Unless someone is in danger, I will never yell. That's a short, easy-to-remember sentence – but pre-deciding that he wanted to model calm and reasoned communication to his students has paid ample dividends. They notice quickly that his classrooms run very differently, and the respect he affords them is almost always reciprocated, he reports. When you make intentional values decisions that affect the way others in the organization experience their day, you help others reach for the stars, too – consciously or subconsciously. I'm not saying this makes everything easy, but it makes everything easier to sort out, deal with, understand, and execute, bit by bit.

Strategy 4: Encourage situational heroes who personify the culture, its values, and important principles. Organizations worldwide, whether they are government, private, technology-driven, medical or legal, engineering, and so on, need cultures with vitality and optimism. Situational heroes are people who rise to the occasion and embrace change. They don't hesitate to leap into uncharted territory. They help blaze new trails and remain enthusiastic for what lies ahead. These are our situational heroes, and when you discover one, enable that person to take the lead somewhere. It is not about managing people, it is about managing intellectual capital and infusing your company's culture with humble actions, optimum behavior, courage to do the right thing, and servant leadership. Situational heroes shape and fine-tune an organization's culture on a people-to-people basis, from the heart. And heart counts when it comes to creating a dynamic culture.

Looking through the lens of media, people sometimes think that a hero is a person with great charisma, good looks, and overwhelming presence. On the contrary: Situational leaders come in all shapes and sizes. Some are quiet and shy, and some are hard-nosed and bold. They represent a wide variety of people and personalities. Charisma is not a requisite of the job description.

Strategy 5: Establish annual events and rituals of the organization – this is culture in action.

Rites and rituals of an organization automatically provide an effective vehicle of ongoing communication among workers. Storytelling is always at play, and the story of your organization is told intentionally through events, such as annual company picnics, a leader's state-of-the-organization address, sales contests, awards banquets, and more. Honor employees who inspire innovation to get more of it. Ceremonies and traditions are to the organization what music is to dance, or the protagonist is to a novel. They go together. They enhance impact.

Examples of culture-driven traditions and rituals might include the following:

- Sales contests
- Employee of the year award
- Softball or soccer teams, or any sports team
- New-hire onboarding
- Retreats
- Annual strategic planning sessions
- Verbal chants, like "Go team, Apollo!"
- Community involvement and charitable causes
- Banquets
- Costume parties

Whether it's a cultural extravaganza or hitting a specific milestone, traditions help build pride and encourage results.

Leadership Is Challenged When Cultures Merge

It's not unusual for cultures to merge. We see it in every area of business, from airlines to healthcare companies, insurance companies to grocery stores, and even law firms. In the modern era, it's not at all unusual for two business cultures to be combined in a blink. When this happens, typically there are three possible directions that the SHIFTS process will take place. It's important to be aware of these SHIFTS.

1. Survival of the fittest prevails. Whenever there is a dominant culture, the less dominant culture is expected to adopt the stronger culture's way of doing things.

2. When east meets west and north meets south – but no one yields. This happens when cultures merge but decide to maintain separate identities. This can be a good thing if the cultures are so polarized that keeping things separate benefits the stakeholders and shareholders. If one culture is young, tattooed, and wearing shorts to work, but the other is more traditional on appearance and mentality, then keeping culture identity separate might be a good bet.

3. When cultures blend. Yes. This happens, too. Two cultures can blend with one another when they extract the best of both cultures for the most desirable outcomes. One way this is done is to benchmark systems and processes against each other with a desire to improve the overall system and procedures. One example might be to take the human resources system from one company and the technology system from the other company and blend them together.

The leaders in organizations involved in mergers bear the primary responsibility of managing the cultural change process. Edgar Schein outlines four critical tasks for leaders in the cultural change process during a merger.[5] First, leaders must understand their own culture well enough to detect where it will be incompatible with those of the partner organization. Second, leaders must be able to decipher the culture of the other organization. Third, leaders must be able to articulate the potential compatibilities and incompatibilities in such a way that those involved can deal with the cultural realities. And, if the leader of the change process in either organization is not a CEO, they must be able to persuade the CEO to prioritize cultural issues. Schein further identified qualities required of leaders who can stimulate cultural learning. These include perception and insight that help the leader to spot and understand cultural problems, motivation, emotional strength, ability to change the cultural assumptions, and ability to create involvement and participation.

Don't Force It

You can't force culture, so don't try. However, you can infuse positive change and opportunity into the work environment and thereby influence creative new approaches for everyone. That's a shift. Culture is always going to be the culmination of your organization's values, traditions, languages, processes, personalities, and more. Your company's leadership – good or bad – is the most powerful and influential force to improve and make things better. Leadership SHIFTS create the right conditions in which culture is encouraged to flourish. SHIFTS do not create culture itself.

The SHIFTS we make harness brainpower. That's crucial. When your leaders learn to use the organization's culture effectively, it will become the most stable part of its future success, especially in a multicultural and multigenerational world. And that takes me to our next section, "Multigenerational SHIFTS." If ever there was a time for productive mind shifts it is now.

Multigenerational SHIFTS

One beautiful morning, I struck up a conversation with a gentleman sitting next to me on an early morning flight from Atlanta to New York. We quickly established common ground when he mentioned that he was an engineer. I shared with him that I had also trained in engineering. When he discovered I was an executive leadership coach, he quickly inquired about my thoughts on general employee attitudes, age gaps, behaviors in the workplace, and specifically how job performance related to us as leaders and to younger generations. It was clear to me that he was looking for ways to close the generational divide. I know that feeling. I let him know I'd researched and written about this topic for numerous publications and in some of my books. He appreciated me sharing this and offered to listen. The flight attendant passed by with a cart and we continued our talk.

He recalled a few of his own experiences, finally saying, a bit in frustration, "There was a time when we started work at 9 a.m. and closed when the job was done, which was usually later than 5 p.m." I could tell he was still stuck in a time long gone and with attitudes that no longer applied in the way they once did. Job performance and results are no longer measured the same way, but he did not seem to fully accept this concept. He went on to pass judgment that today's younger workers might start working at 8 a.m. or 9 a.m. and then seemingly can't wait for it to be quitting time. I understood his frustration, but these are new times, and personally, I disagree with his perception because younger workers now connect the amount of time they spend to the task required; if they've completed the day's tasks at 1:00, why should they stay in the office for four more hours? It's a new mindset. It's a new day. Performance and results are no longer measured by minutes on the clock. They're measure by pure excellence, results, creativity, and all in service of the most efficient profitable outcomes.

I asked him if he understood that these cultural shifts had happened because the world is so different now from what we knew when we were younger. I suggested there were many factors. Rather than rattle off statistics on performance and multigenerational teams, I focused on one area and suggested how the entertainment industry, for example, could be playing a huge role of influence. This seemed more interesting than just a bunch of stats or a lecture on how times have shifted.

Entertainment and Influential SHIFTS

We discussed how at one time, decades ago, television broadcasts had start and stop times and channels were limited. I know this resonates as "old school" but it's a relatable guidepost, and certainly one he understood. The concept of three major networks no longer exists. And that's a good thing. No, it's a great thing.

Obviously, today television news is 24/7 and there are hundreds of news channels in most countries. And although you can still go to the cinema to watch movies, you can also watch movies whenever you want to on Netflix and other networks – at home, in your hotel room, and on all your mobile devices. Your kids are doing this, too.

Then there's virtual reality. It takes you to the top of the Swiss mountains or the bottom of the deepest ocean. All of this is relatable to generational divides. These divides will continue to expand even more. I look back and I must laugh at the TV sitcoms we enjoyed in our youth. They aired for 30 minutes only once a week. You had to wait a full week to watch another episode. Can you imagine waiting a week to see anything now? Can you imagine waiting a full minute? Incomprehensible! That's a shift. Today we simply binge watch. Speed of information is key. Heck, speed-everything is key . . . speed dating, rapid medical testing, faster forms of transportation, and speed mentoring. By the time you read this chapter, I might be sitting on another planet. I'm just kidding, but you get the point. As I type this, a SpaceX mission is enabling a billionaire to take the first private space walk in human history, something no one would have thought possible just 20 years ago. The need for speed is not just for *Top Gun* movie enthusiasts, it's a cultural force that now affects every one of us, every moment of the day. The speed at which you choose to move is up to you, but the speed at which we shift – generation to generation – is here to stay.

How can we apply the SHIFTS model across generations while being sensitive to the differences between them? Our responsibility is not to encounter and conquer. It is to encounter, listen, and appreciate all our differences. The SHIFTS model applies to all ages and stages of life. It's the application of each step that each of us is responsible for tweaking to fit the needs of the group involved. The message might be the same, but how it is used might look different if you're 20 or 70. Remember, at the beginning of this book I emphasized the importance of adapting and modifying the information in this book to fit your unique leadership style and performance methods.

Generational gap leadership is complex and often a dilemma. Not everyone is going to think like you do. And isn't that a good thing? The world would be boring if we were all the same and innovative thinking would most likely come to a halt.

Wisdom Is Not Governed by Age

Some years back, we hosted a get-together that we named The Leadership Edge Conference at New York City, but I became uncomfortable after we hosted the second edition in Chicago. The results, though good, did not seem to justify the huge resources committed to the conference. I reflected deeply on it one morning, exploring alternatives for making greater impact with less expense, when the idea occurred to me to run the event online. The next time, we hosted the event on Facebook. It was attended by hundreds of people from over 30 countries. All it cost was for me to sit by my laptop and to connect to the Wi-Fi at the office. I could not contain my excitement. When it was over, my marketing consultant, Harriett Burrell, congratulated me and asked if we could talk over a cup of coffee. She explained gently that she had been trying to get me to see the value in pushing our content online, especially promoting it on social media. At that point, I remembered how she had asked me to hold my camera and to record myself on video sharing useful information. I confessed to her that I recorded two videos, felt awkward looking at myself, and never presented those videos to her. She smiled and said that she understood, and that it had to do with age. She said if she were me, she would hire a young man in his 20s, give him a good phone, and get him to follow me around the world recording me. Then she and her team would post the content on my behalf. It was a paradigm-shifting moment for me.

Not long after that, our son, David, graduated from college. I proposed for him to come do what Harriett had suggested at our office and he agreed. For a start, we gave him 27-minute videos from our *Success Power* television broadcast. He cut them up into smaller videos that were less than 60 seconds. The effect was dramatic when we posted them on social media. We quickly recorded over 10,000 likes, then it went up to 15,000, and then over 20,000. This is the power cross-generations are using and we love it. I learned a big lesson. We shortchange ourselves when we don't leverage multiple perspectives and skills across generations. This reminds me of the famous David and Goliath story. If David's leader and king, Saul, had not listened to David and allowed him to test his ideas, the whole nation would have been compromised. What a great cross-generational story.

SHIFTS on both sides are required of leaders in a multigenerational workplace. This is the key that enables us to unleash our greatest successes and welcome inclusion. Ideas vetted by a diverse group of leaders almost always will be stronger than any ideas offered up by people of identical backgrounds and upbringings. Wisdom is not governed by age, but instead it's driven by sheer knowledge and what's now being referred to as speed mentoring.

Speed Mentoring

We've spent decades trying to formalize mentorship. Yes, it's a process, but it can be less stuffy, as they say. Speed mentoring includes a mutual mentoring approach and often takes place in a group setting. Young people talk about their issues. They address mental health concerns, they talk about communication barriers, how they were raised, and where they want to be. This approach is relatively new generationally, but it is critical if we are to start closing generational gaps and holes.

There's something to be gained with this approach, on both sides. Chip Conley, the popular author and renowned hotelier, knows a few things about knowledge transfer and speed mentoring. He coined the term *modern elder*, or *modern mentor*. It describes senior coaches who share their knowledge but are also open to receiving knowledge and feedback from their youngest counterparts without insecurity factoring in. What a fresh idea!

In years past, we viewed mentoring as a one-way street. The seasoned professional took college grads under their wings to help develop their skill sets. But now, more baby boomers are reverting to the workplace after retirement and desperately need support and assistance from a more current generation of technological gurus and intuitive leaders. The younger generation is composed of the speed mentors. What a great opportunity to close the gap and move forward together. It all requires a new mindset and several mind SHIFTS.

Five Generations Working Side by Side

Five generations are working together under the same roofs. Can you believe it? It's the first time this has ever happened in the history of the global workforce. With this comes great learning and growth opportunity for everyone involved. Are you making the most of the situation or are you staying stuck in old ways? As age becomes more and more attention-getting, we need to make important leadership SHIFTS and bridge the generational divide. Never in the history of the world have there been so many generations working together, which creates great opportunities to make leadership SHIFTS and apply the model in this book.

What are the five generations? Traditionalists, baby boomers, generation X, millennials, and generation Z. Yes, it's one big happy family! Seriously, this scenario has caused some frustration within the generational divide and understandably so. Twenty-year-old workers on teams with workers over 60 years old can make for an enormous clash of different views and perspectives. However, there's a remarkable, positive side to this new way of working and leading that no one can deny. And I'll gladly add one more generation here for good measure: generation next. I can hardly wait.

> Across all the generations there is as much for each of us to learn as there is to teach others.
> —Sam Adeyemi

Workers are incentivized to remain relevant, keep up, and move at quicker speed. Gen X started in the workforce in 2010. Millennials make up almost 4% of the total workforce. So, what will the future look like as a result? Projections indicate that by 2030 millennials and gen Zs will become half of the entire workforce.[6] This gives them a special opportunity to mentor and guide younger workers, while simultaneously addressing their own deficiencies and upgrading their skill sets. It's mutually beneficial. And seeking mutual benefit is what closing the generational gap requires. Modern elders are holding the generational golden ticket for more than just one group.

Forget the Age of Your Teammates and Just Mentor Someone

Regardless of your age or stage of your career, focus on dedicating time to help someone. Here are some ways to get started as a speed mentor:

1. Seek out people, no matter what their age, whom you can assist with your knowledge and background and look for ways that they can assist you, too. Perhaps it's in the technology arena, or a system you've been studying, or just an attitude about the person sitting next to you who looks different and speaks different. Strong mentors help others get to know people and understand why they express themselves the way they do. They shift paradigms. Look past the façade and focus on the person. Ask for help.

2. State your respective goals and what you're aiming for. Allow for a healthy exchange of new ideas and perspectives, even in your own area of expertise and accomplishment. All of us can get better. There's always room for improvement no matter what your status or level of accomplishment. This is a good time to get over yourself.

3. Outline your goals. Have the other person outline their goals. Now, how can you help each other to get to where you want to be?

4. What stories can you share that will motivate or inspire the other person? Everyone has a story (and there's always a story behind the story, as well). This is information you can't access online, in a textbook, or in a new-hire orientation or onboarding session. It's the human condition, and a piece of this knowledge can be a brilliant path forward.

5. Carve out time from your busy schedule. It might be a simple phone call or voice message, a text, or stopping by to see someone spontaneously. Show you care. Then stop talking and listen.

6. Acknowledge that team members are not just cogs in the wheel. Make everyone feel part of the bigger picture. Show them how to use their diverse generational traits to serve a common purpose to help your organization achieve success.

7. Acknowledge that all leaders started at a lower-level position at one time. Every one of us. Multigenerational workplaces give back to one another. When a person succeeds due to mentoring, they will forever be touched and influenced by that person. It will help shape the mentor they are to become. It becomes one success story after another. Be a memory maker. Be cooperative. Be grateful.

8. Accept and appreciate that not everyone is like you. Thank goodness!

If you're a seasoned mentor and want to get better, stop referring to when you were younger and how things were done in the old days. Frankly, no one cares. Look through people into their hearts, minds, and souls. Remember how you were as a young person. Feel it. Stop passing judgment and start making good judgment, and only tell stories about the old days when there's a clear benefit or application to the issue at hand. I have a real-world example to share.

A friend of mine who became a successful author and speaker told me about a time when she mentored a young

(continued)

(continued)

man in New York City who did not fit the accepted profile of many men who might become successful entrepreneurs and eventually family oriented. Twenty-five years younger than she, the young man was tattooed on most of his body and had body piercings and spoke with a heavy Latin accent. My friend told me that she only saw this as a "life expression." She said, "We all go through things in life where we express ourselves and it sticks with us. People make fast judgments and stay away from a young man like this with all the potential in the world. Mentors see the potential."

Every one of us has had life experiences. We all express them differently in our youth. Sometimes people get artwork tattooed on their bodies, or they act out, or they gamble their rent money, or they just don't know where to turn. No one knows your story. It's called being human. Mentors see the inside of a person, as well as the outside. Like Superman, have a sort of x-ray vison into human potential and authenticity, refusing to be sidetracked by focusing on appearances alone.

For five years my friend mentored this young man, who became a very successful entrepreneur selling electronics. He also became a responsible and dedicated husband and father and went on to speed mentor my friend when she needed new technology in her home and comforted her in times of sadness when her family experienced loss. He continues to this day to be available and helpful to her and her family. That's a life-changing speed mentor. No judgment. Just compassion. She helped him. And he helped her. Sometimes you've got to See and Hear deeper than the obvious. That opens your heart to Insights and to Formulate and Transform life changes that can lead a person to Succeed. This is your SHIFTS formula at work.

It's time to build a bridge and get over the generational divide. Following are some leadership tips that I believe bring multigenerational workplaces closer:

- Build a culture of trust.
- Sustain top talent.
- Appreciate unique differences.
- Promote a cohesive workplace.
- Use your unique voice to communicate with each generation.
- Support generational values as they evolve.
- Accommodate differences when possible.
- Be flexible in your leadership style.
- Respect and honor competence, willingness to learn, and initiative.
- Be the bridge maker you expect others to be and keep minding the gaps, big and small.

Being aware of generational difference enables us to assist those around us and enhance their maximum effect. Great businesses are built on understanding others' perspectives and values. We're not all the same, but we can share empathy. Embrace generational uniqueness while keeping your organization's mission and vision at the helm. Remember that a multigenerational workforce has great benefits:

- Different viewpoints that create well-rounded behaviors
- Younger people who can tap resources and question outdated processes

- Older generations who can be a support system with awesome people skills to teach younger employees who might lack such "soft skills"

Together, everyone can create an environment of collaboration in a multigenerational, multicultural work environment serving the needs of many across the miles. This organically leads us to our next topic, the importance of working from a distance and the SHIFTS required to connect our multigenerational society together across every ocean and continent. Here we go.

> Every generation imagines itself to be more intelligent
> than the one before it and the one that comes after it.
> —George Orwell

Keep in mind, age is only how many times the earth has revolved around the sun in one's lifetime. Take time to examine and appreciate one-of-a-kind traits, attitudes, and workstyles. They are each rich within their own styles of business and human growth development. Communicate and coach each other. I'll share a piece of me, if you share a piece of you. And we'll both be glad we did.

Distance SHIFTS: How Working from 6,000 Miles Away Elevated Bigger, Bolder Mind Shifts

I was reading through the reports of our church activities for the previous week when I observed something unusual. We had about 15,000 unique connections or people attending events on our website and social media platforms during our regular Sunday scheduled events. That was a truly huge crowd.

When I checked the reports several weeks back, the numbers had grown steadily without us paying attention. This all took place about two years before COVID-19 started up. I brought up the matter for discussion at our management meeting. I challenged our team to make SHIFTS in attitude toward those individuals participating in our church events online. We were accustomed to referring to participants as our online audience. However, this needed to shift immediately. In my view, these people were not *spectators*. They were as much participants as those physically present. We knew if we could Formulate a new approach, our belief systems could create new decisions and habits. Like the model shows, we could then transform our actions and thoughts for bigger, bolder moves with everyone included.

We had extensive discussions on the participation of those that attend our services online. Not only did we shift our attitude, but we also designed a cultural distance shift. With the large number of people attending online, we designated our online program as one of our campuses. Thinking about it in terms of a physical campus, rather than a disembodied space in the cloud, was a pivotal shift in our thinking. We appointed a pastoral head for the online campus with a mandate to recruit volunteers. The volunteers would engage people online 5 to 10 minutes before the start of an event and join the event once it started. We welcomed attendees online to the event before we welcomed those present in person. When we provide cards to first-time guests to share their information with us, we also provide a link for those in the chat room and a QR code on the screen. At the end of the event, there's a switch back to

Professional SHIFTS (Team, Multigenerational, Distance)

the studio where the anchors engage the online community, providing feedback from various social media platforms before they end the event.

This experience involved shifting perspectives, creating new units (these are departments where volunteers serve with their best skills, helping recruit and train volunteers), and learning new behaviors. Many generously donate electronically to keep the program going strong. People value our chat rooms and the access they provide to support and new ideas. It was all worthwhile. Believe it or not, our attendance online grew past the physical attendance we had in just a matter of months – and this all happened *before* the COVID-19 pandemic. This meant that when the pandemic occurred, our intentional self-disruption had already positioned us for excellence in executing online events.

Remember how in the process model we talk about the *S* in Succeed? This is where your actions lead to greater satisfaction and success. Shifting to online-only events was seamless for us. Jumping into the opportunity to lead from a distance was the best thing that could have ever happened. Yes, it was scary at first, but then we watched as our teams excelled in their individual leadership styles. The lesson was that sometimes we need to self-disrupt to ride the winds of change. Our decision set us sailing forward with pride. Here's how we adapted and set sail for getting comfortable with distance leadership techniques. I'm confident this mindset will help you, as well.

Set Sail for Distance Leadership

Imagine yourself on a sailboat on a lake. The sailboat does not have any engine to power it, and the waves can rock the boat, making you feel unsteady. It occurs to you that you do not have control over the forces that control the movement of your sailboat. For example, without any wind, you cannot move toward your destination. You cannot control the speed of the wind, the direction of the wind, or the force of the wind. But you realize that as you drive the sailboat, you do have control over the sail. And so, here is a critical mind shift to take note of. When you control the sail, the wind that you cannot control can take you to where you want to go. This is a huge awakening and a parallel for life. You must eventually come to a point where you accept that you cannot control everything. None of us can, but when we focus our energy on things that we cannot control, it is like signing a contract with perpetual frustration or defeat. What control do you have over the wind or the weather? Or the opinions of other people? Or unforeseen transformations you might eventually face? None. So control what you can, and adapt to what you cannot.

Working Remotely Challenges Leaders to Think Differently

External forces that you cannot influence challenge you to think or behave in a different way. I have experienced this for decades in my own business's growth and SHIFTS. I wrote this book so that you will be even better prepared to make the SHIFTS necessary when it comes to leading from afar. When we are faced with these external forces, thinking outside traditional or habitual norms and using creativity to figure out new ways to make things work requires a mind shift, which particularly applies to working remotely. When you shift your thoughts and mindsets, they become the foundation for many upcoming situations. Your thoughts are extremely powerful. Thoughts influence your decision-making and behavior.

Professional SHIFTS (Team, Multigenerational, Distance)

Thoughts become conscious, and here is where you do have control. Only you control your thoughts, enabling them to manifest better results. And you will always be able to control how you respond to situations that are totally out of your control, whether that be unforeseen financial circumstances, worldwide pandemics, unhealthy relationships, personal sicknesses, other people's viewpoints or choices, and more. Only you can put a framework for how you respond and bond to people and life's situations 10 feet away, or 10,000 miles away. Successful remote leadership SHIFTS speak to these concerns and considerations.

A few years ago, with little warning, a great many people all over the world were faced with the sudden challenge of leading from a distance. The pandemic required a huge shift of thoughts and behaviors for many leaders. Making your presence felt from a distance – be it thousands of miles or even just one block – can be critical to the success of any business. Communications skills are critical. I have experienced this from across the globe, and it can be a very lonely feeling as a leader. Building bonding relationships from a distance – when entire businesses and employees' livelihoods are at stake – is a tall order, even for the most equipped and celebrated of leaders.

Leading from a distance became a priority for a time, then we ushered back onsite working conditions. When employees started to resign or were laid off, we fell back to remote work teams, but many quickly tried to force the values of our old workplaces into a new context, without realizing that we as leaders would only be met halfway. Those who managed the transition well did so because they acknowledged that we had to become leaders for all seasons and reasons, no matter where we worked from.

I think a big challenge for leaders is shifting their ways of doing things and their thoughts toward managing from a distance. But you can't transform mindsets without doing so. Psychologically, it creates a sort of abyss. But once you have the facts and learn the techniques, you can close that gap. The research shows that employees are more productive and efficient when they can lead and work from anywhere. They feel empowered. According to the Pew Research Center, among workers who can, about one-third now work from home permanently, and about 40% work on a hybrid schedule – working in the office a set number of days per month and working the rest from home.[7] Working remotely certainly has its perks: no commuting time or costs, no dress code requirements, time flexibility, reduced interruptions, and most important, an improved work-life balance. However, there's no breakroom chats or face-to-face meetings with your colleagues when you work from a distance. How can a leader manage without daily, in-person meetings? How do they tackle day-to-day challenges, better approach productivity and morale, and help employees to avoid burnout or boredom? Other concerns run deeper, like avoiding distractions when trying to get the job done, failing to listen carefully to instruction because you're not in person, imagining negativity and making judgments, team politics from remote locations, or even losing sight of the company's work ethics.

Managing a remote team comes with unique challenges: figuring out how best to keep lines of communication open, connecting with coworkers, forming a cohesive team who works well together, and facing fewer opportunities to connect on a personal level. In my years of managing remote teams in multiple locations, I've learned some tried-and-true ways to best manage a team from a distance.

Professional SHIFTS (Team, Multigenerational, Distance)

Learn to Adapt

Leading from a distance requires that we as leaders willingly learn to adapt our ways. When you adapt to new circumstances, you change the expectations of your followers and the entire workplace culture. But doing so can be much more difficult than it appears. So how will we get there? I've put together these eight tips on how leaders can shift and improve distance leadership and remote guidance.

1. Be empathetic from afar. Show a genuine interest in others wherever they live or work. It's not just about your city, or your office headquarters, or your team's specialty. It's about leading anyone from anywhere. Show you care. People know when their leadership is authentic or phony. They sense it. If people feel there is a façade at play, they know they will not be heard and they will resign or, even worse, hang around while ignoring their leadership. The world saw this in the early days of the NASA program. Astronauts were working in space but empathy and concern for their greatest well-being was not being felt as time went on. As a result, there were many incidents and even tragedies on various missions. Decisions were made that were in the best interest of a competitive space race and government public relations. Today's space projects, both government and private, show great empathy for the families of astronauts and the astronauts' ultimate safety and well-being, mental health, and so on. A genuine interest is felt in space aviation on earth and outside of it as a result. Authentic leadership is a mind shift. It's intentional. And when it's felt, it will always have a positive impact from any distance because workers feel leadership's commitment and the desire to perform at higher

levels, whenever and however possible. The shift is palpable when this occurs. Without empathy and authenticity, you will miss the mark with both people and profits.

2. Develop your own company culture's ways to communicate. All organizations are different. Ask the people in the field, "How would you like leadership to communicate with you? What resources will you need to be successful from a distance? What is your preferred style of communication? What communication process do you recommend based on your experience in this area?" Distance leadership looks different everywhere. Rules and regulations shift if you're assigned to a post in Western Europe versus the western United States, Asia or Antarctica, Boseman, Montana, or Budapest. Also, remember that each generation has its own communication style. Ask for feedback on each unique group of workers and take time to learn how to communicate across the divide. It's done every day, but you must be willing to do it. Beyond that, every person you lead is an individual with a more pronounced nuance. How you relate to them one-on-one matters a lot. Address people by their names and individually on video calls and in meetings when possible. It's true that human beings respond positively to the sound of their own names when they are being spoken to. They feel heard and valued, and that crosses all geographic boundaries.

3. Welcome inclusion and diversity. Embrace inclusion and diversity on a wide scale. Be genuine in your efforts. Take time to learn about other people's way of doing things. Find out how people learn best and what they respect and honor. We are one humanity. The most successful leaders take time to make the SHIFTS necessary to better

(continued)

(continued)

understand the differences of the people they lead. Inclusion is a watershed moment for the working world. As we discuss in Chapter 6, never have there been so many generations from so many different families and ethnicities in one global workplace environment. And there are more to come. The most successful leaders make it a priority to embrace the uniqueness of humankind within their teams and organizations.

4. Reward people from a distance. Build ambassadorships worldwide. Internal ambassadors are people who protect your organization's one-of-a-kind culture, recognize and reward employees, look for the best – not the worst – in others, celebrate successes, learn from failures, and make new hires feel welcome by reinforcing what everyone has to look forward to by being a part of the organization. When these things are practiced from a distance, everyone gets excited about what's to come.

5. Hiring questions for possible remote teammates: "Do you consider yourself a good communicator? Why? Explain. Give me a specific example of when you shifted the course of activity to elevate leadership. Do you think of yourself as an effective collaborator? When have you collaborated with a distance team and influenced results that continue? And for what period?" And last, "What motivates you to be your best? Please be specific." (A remote worker might answer, "A job well done, monetary compensation, benefits and perks for my family, opportunity for advancement," etc.) Asking these hiring questions for a remote and distance worker will provide insight to what they consider most important and how they will complement your

workplace culture. Now it's your job to make the match. Hire to match the culture you exemplify. Life will be easier when you do.

6. Remote workers must be excellent listeners. There's a program called the *Dichotic Listening Test*. It is a straight-forward exam. The listener puts on headphones and the right ear plays one thing and the left ear plays another. Participants are instructed to only listen to one side and ignore the other. It's interesting how closely this applies to leaders dealing with remote teammates. Consciously or subconsciously, they will listen to what interests them the most or is easiest, but they might ignore any voices that require difficulty or might shake up the organization's way of doing things. Leaders who lead from afar with passion and gusto never stop listening to both sides. They might not acknowledge or agree with every point, but they are paying close attention to those near and far, ensuring everyone is heard and respected.

7. Provide a safe space remotely. Appreciate differences and support varying values of individuals. Even in the most harmonious workplaces you will find conflict or confrontation (confrontation is not conflict, but simply two distinctly different ideas coming together at once and examining all the options; it's a good thing, not a bad thing, as some might assume). Ideological disagreements do not have to equate to real-life fighting. Support a wide range of value systems but create safe spaces for people to agree to disagree in open dialogue and across every continent. Set the example. What happens in an organization is often the direct reflection of its leadership team in one way or another. Practice what you preach, as they say.

(continued)

(continued)

8. Mind the gaps. Not every employee can automatically rise to the challenge. Yes, there are those who have an innate desire and ability to influence, but there are others who might well become your greatest workplace champions. These yet-to-be-discovered superstars will be motivated by your examples of leadership. Gallup polls have revealed that as much as 70% of employee behavior comes from modeling the leader in an organization.[8] Don't expect remote workers to build all the bridges if you as their leader are not prepared to build your own and walk across it.

A Few Fun Facts Our Organizations Learned Along the Way

- You can increase your company's profit when you mind the gaps and increase engagement activities.

- Be curious. Stay curious.

- Measure the gap between what you say and what you do when leading remotely. It's easier to just say things or make promises when leading from a distance. Success comes from doing what you say you will do.

- Keep defining and redefining your culture. It deserves all the attention you can give it.

- Identify your organization's priorities and ultimate goals. Now hire the talent that exemplifies all the characteristics and traits to make it all happen. Be the possibility.

- Remote workers invite leaders to return to reminders of their purpose, vision, and mission. Keep these ideas top-of-mind.

- Let your distance workers become mini-incubators for new ideas and improvement. Remember, they see and are exposed to things you are not.

- Assume everyone is a visionary.

- Articulate what you want as a leader. Repeat what your workers want. This helps close the gap. If a worker wants a raise, talk about it. If someone is unhappy on the job, talk about it.

- Your belief system is not a superstition. All organizations have spoken and unspoken rules that drive behavior. Bring the two together and eliminate the guessing games.

- Ask some of these questions regularly of your remote workers: "What does it mean to you to be part of a group that is spread across different countries? What do you tolerate that you wish you didn't have to? How does it feel to work together but apart? How can we better treat our remote teammates? Looking at things from a distance, how would you describe your value to the organization and your specific team or customers?"

Ask yourself: Do you want to do a job for this organization, or do you want to make a real difference and change the course for a better tomorrow? This can also become a personal declaration that helps people make critical and important SHIFTS in both their personal and professional lives. You have a chance to help make that a reality for your people. Hope, such as that discussed by Barack Obama, can change the perpetuity of an entire global initiative. Channel all the resources you have and provide hope, not just for distance workers, but for everyone, including yourself.

Leading from almost anywhere requires that you somehow leave an imprint on your team. This doesn't mean stalking your team. In most cases, organizational leaders should not be reaching out to employees for connection purposes. Let the team leaders and managers do that. No one wants to feel like the top bosses are watching them or stalking them, especially online. This, of course, would not be your intention, but how the actions are interpreted might create a different reaction. Similarly, if an employee reaches out to a leader, the leader can respond, update, or delete any updates. Apply what you do uniformly. And be very careful what you document or post for all to see. One moment of frustration can become a lifetime of regret. Use the SHIFTS model. The SHIFTS you make toward honesty, values, empathy, sincerity, and self-integrity will always equal top leadership standards and behaviors, which are all addressed in this book. Empowered leaders establish regular communication, leverage technology, make their presence felt, trust others, empower their teams, hire for talent and attitude, use transparency, and appreciate or acknowledge the contributions, hardships, successes, and reasonable desires of those on their team.

It's a New Era – Distance Leadership Is Here to Stay

There's no denying it. We're in a new era of distance leadership and remote work. Stats continue to show that people can be more effective and productive when allowed to work from home. The stress is off their shoulders. There are no subways to ride or work clothes and special makeup to buy. Freedom like this can be awesome for so many, but leaders must learn how to lead from afar. Many feel their control is lost. Trust is at stake. Leaders sometimes feel less important or looked up to. It all makes sense. It's human behavior. But let's face it, the workers have spoken, and remote work is here to stay. The question is, will leaders be able to lead in this new environment or will it take an entirely new group of leaders, or a new generation of leadership, to step in and make it work better than it did before when people came to the office and worked from 9 to 5?

The 21st-century transformational leader learns quickly how to leverage the following illuminating insights so that they can lead from a distance effectively, keeping the team engaged and helping workers to strike a new balance in their work and personal life. Here's a collection of ideas and tips that have worked for me and my teams.

Establish Regular Communication

If communication weren't important enough in a traditional office setting, then it is significantly more important when working with off-site teams. I'll go as far as to say it's the backbone of a team. Constant communication among a team is vital for its success. Without regular communication, you run the risk of creating information silos, having details fall through the cracks, or making duplicative efforts.

Establishing regular communication with teams helps ensure they remain connected, facilitates working together effectively, and can even boost productivity and morale. Celebrating the little wins like hitting milestones or even sharing a laugh can foster a sense of community on your team. Effective communication enables leaders to stay attuned to any roadblocks and monitor project status. Unlike fine wine, bad news does not improve with age. If you do not know what is happening on your team, you cannot provide help and guidance if it is needed.

Professional SHIFTS (Team, Multigenerational, Distance)

Everyone on the team is on an even level when they have all the information. Proactive communication is essential.

Leverage Technology

We are fortunate to live in an age when the ability to earn a living by working remotely is a possibility. Multiple online technologies were created for streamlining communication and engaging teams, in and out of the traditional office setting. Using platforms like Microsoft Teams, Zoom, Slack, Trello, Monday.com, and other tools including email, text, and group chats can pave the way toward team unity. The leader is responsible for ensuring each person knows what the preferred methods of communication are among the team, where to share or store files, and how to navigate the technology. But be sure to be mindful of potential pitfalls, such as communicating tone over text and instant messages.

Also remember that the technology playing field is not level. There are multiple generations in the workforce today, which we've already discussed. Lots of people start at different levels of comfort and knowledge when it comes to learning and using a new technology. It might take one person longer to understand how a file sharing drive works or how to use an online collaboration tool. A good leader will ensure their team has access to plenty of training on how to use their team's chosen technology. Be patient and it will pay off.

Make Your Presence Felt

It is essential for a leader to create a strong sense of connection and presence on their teams. Smart leaders begin by setting the tone of the team and defining what and how members collaborate and interact. After all, as the saying goes, a fish rots from the head. You should model the behavior you wish to see on your team, which sets the expectation for others to follow. This includes embracing new technology or processes that will help you connect with your team. Hold regular one-on-one meetings with your team members, during which you have a conversation about work but also about nonwork things, such as pop culture, hobbies, or sports. Let your values and empathy guide you. Demonstrate your integrity, follow through with intentions, and provide a supportive presence to whom your team can turn with questions or concerns.

During online meetings every minute counts, making it challenging to achieve connections that would otherwise be made during face-to-face encounters. You can take a personal interest in your teammates and show you genuinely care about their growth as a professional and as a human being. Showing a personal interest in the people you work with goes a long way, as I've said previously, but only if it is honest and sincere. I am not saying that you should be intrusive toward your colleagues; by showing you are a kind and caring leader, you speak volumes about not only your empathy but also about building loyalty and unity on your team. Remembering what people share shows you are not just phoning it in. Your personal touch can help people feel connected. Everyone has a story and there's always a story behind the story. Don't make negative assumptions about anyone. Instead, choose to operate from the assumption that everyone is trying to do their best work as efficiently as possible. The question is, will you help them, hinder them, or harm them? The last two options are unacceptable.

Trust Lessens Isolation

Trust is a pillar of the foundation for leading from a distance because it cultivates a collaborative and productive work culture and environment. Research shows that people who work remotely can be more productive. Prioritizing and promoting trust on your team can create a resilient team that can weather any unforeseen challenge. Add in regular and consistent communication along with trust, and you get a cohesive team that feels comfortable collaborating, brainstorming, and voicing concerns in a safe and respectful atmosphere.

Trust can also help lessen the isolation that remote teams might experience by fostering a sense of community and connectivity. When a team is supportive of its members, they are more likely to stay committed to their roles and be engaged. Team members trust one another to be accountable so everyone can work toward shared goals. A connected team promotes a sense of belonging and unity.

Seventy-nine percent of adults who work from a distance say they feel trusted by their leader.[9] Feeling trusted empowers autonomy and motivates a team to take ownership of their projects. A leader who trusts their team is less likely to micromanage, which might boost a team's confidence, risk-taking, abilities, decision-making, and morale. A culture of trust can build a strong and unified team that hits goals and enjoys working together. Trust is a vital part of teams that thrive.

Empower Your Team

Empowerment is another cornerstone of good team leadership. By delegating responsibility and authority, a leader grants autonomy to their team members so they can make decisions and take initiative and ownership of their work. Smart leaders trust the decisions of their teams and encourage team members to take initiative. When team members are trusted to do their job, they can feel they are making a meaningful contribution that is valued and appreciated. And as a bonus, this can also foster a positive work culture.

An empowered team knows what is expected of them. They know their lane, when to hand off the baton to another team member, and when to ask for help. Without constant intervention or micromanagement, team members are free to unlock their unlimited potential to be creative and innovative without fear of reprisal. An empowered team is resilient, adaptable, and not hindered by the limitations of others, least of all their team leader.

Hire for Talent

Bringing the right people to a remote team is essential for leading from a distance. It's not all about attitude. Real talent is critical. Hiring boils down to taking a leap of faith after you've done your due diligence for skill. You really don't know someone until you work with them. Trust goes hand-in-hand with hiring for talent. You would not hire a team member whom you do not trust to do the job. The right team members directly shape the cohesiveness, effectiveness, and success of a geographically dispersed team.

If you build a team of people with not only the right skills but also a growth mindset, the sky is the limit. Remote teams must navigate change well; the world of work is continually evolving so learning new work processes and communication protocols, as well as adapting to the technology the team uses, are critical to your team's strength. By finding team members who possess diverse skills and lived experiences, you can create a flexible and versatile team that brings multiple perspectives – and solutions – to the table. Remote team members ideally are intrinsically motivated and can independently juggle a workload with multiple priorities without constant oversight. This trait is vital for being productive and hitting goals in a remote environment.

Team members whose values align with those of the team and organization can make positive contributions and add to a supportive environment that makes everyone feel valued. Creating a high-performing team can make you more competitive in the global landscape. You can achieve excellence and success when you surround yourself with a team that is skilled, unified, and cooperative.

Use Transparency

Being transparent is an essential component of effective leadership for remote teams. Being transparent means promoting open and continual communication, accountability, collaboration, engagement, and trust. These elements are vital when managing a remote team where in-person interactions are somewhat limited. Communicating expectations, goals, and performance metrics of a project encourages accountability and builds trust and team engagement. It makes sense that when you know what your goal is, you can work toward achieving it. Transparent communication helps reduce misunderstandings by making sure everyone is on the same page about objectives, expectations, and any shifts that might arise.

Establishing trust among your team members by sharing information about decisions and how they are made, status updates, and organizational change goes a long way in making them feel included and valued. Trust encourages open dialogue and accountability, both equally important for transparency. When team members understand how their work fits into the big picture, they can engage more and take ownership of their responsibilities.

Transparency can help build collaboration, bridge communication gaps, improve communication, and ensure seamless exchanges of information. Encourage your team to ask questions and answer them to the best of your ability, and use collaboration tools to document every step of every project so nothing gets lost in the handoff from person to person. When everyone has access to the same information, it can promote collaboration so team members can work together toward mutual goals. Nobody works well in a communication void; transparent communication works to remedy that.

Feel Others' Contributions, Hardships, Successes, and Desires

I believe that feeling appreciated falls under the spectrum of self-esteem under Maslow's hierarchy of needs. When we feel appreciated, it hits us in the right emotional spots. On an internal emotional level, we crave feeling appreciated for our efforts, not only at work but at home and elsewhere. Good leaders consistently and sincerely express appreciation to their teams for a job well done to foster a supportive and effective work environment.

Having an awareness of team members' desires and aspirations enables you to align tasks with their strengths, which in turn helps advance job satisfaction and performance. Being an empathetic leader not only grows resilience but also builds a positive team culture, where members feel safe to express themselves and contribute authentically.

Empathy can be taught. If you're a leader, this is your cue. Just remember that teaching empathy requires the employee's willingness to learn and become more empathetic and the leader's commitment to teach and encourage this behavior in others. When both parties commit, attitudes shift and the result becomes an environment in which compassion is valued and empathy SHIFTS from team to team, person to person.

Understanding your team members' individual experiences helps build trust and strengthen the inner workings of your team relationships, further creating a cohesive team dynamic. When people feel valued, they tend to engage more and tap into their inner motivation. Likewise, when a leader recognizes when a team member is struggling and intervenes, they are proactive in preventing burnout and mitigating potential morale issues.

The objective of this chapter is to emphasize that it's important to embrace and not fear distance leadership or remote situations. Distance is as much psychological as it is measurable by miles. Your goal as a leader is to help your people thrive and find the right fit for every person you hire.

Exercise: Multigenerational Application of SHIFTS

Objective: To allow a multigenerational team the space to analyze the current environment in a way that fosters discussion of what could change for the benefit of all team members.

INSTRUCTIONS

See and Hear: Using the SHIFTS model, ask each team member to describe what they See and Hear as they work each day. Are people working together? Are they relaxed and laughing? Do some team members play music at their desks? How is the office decorated? Are things tense? Is there frowning? Do workers exude pride and are they willing to be helpful and considerate? Do people display photos of their families or inspirational quotes? What do people wear to the office?

Insights: What habits, worldviews, or cultural practices do these visual and aural stimuli reveal? Do they reinforce one another, or is there conflict? Are any of these practices out of line with company values held by all? Is it okay to wear traditional clothing from a worker's country and culture? If uniforms are required, how do they make customers feel? Ask someone about the rites and rituals of the organization. What do they enjoy celebrating and why? What are they famous for? Who tells the best stories? Is there a display for any of these fun events? Ask a leader how they think their organization's culture affects their most talented people. Does the organization attract new hires and fresh talent because of its innovative culture? How so? Does the human resources department hire people who are a good match with the cultural environment? Why is that a good thing or wrong thing to do?

Formulate: What practices are appreciated by all? What practices create problems, even if they haven't been verbalized until now? What practices are appreciated as bringing life and joy to the environment, even if no one's pointed that out yet?

Transform: How can the workplace (or online environment) be changed to accommodate each team member without creating friction? What internal shifts might each team member have to make to accept something that feels less than ideal to them personally? Name several things a leader could do to effectively lead a multigenerational team in a shifting culture.

Succeed: Describe what success would look like. How will we know we have made a valuable shift in our thinking in the way we interact with and respond to the other generations we share workspace with?

(continued)

171

(continued)

Outcome: It's not a bad idea to do something like this regularly, at least once a year. Things change faster than ever, and someone fresh out of college often has a completely different set of expectations and values than someone hired fresh out of college just a year ago. By regularly highlighting awareness of multigenerational differences and your commitment to lead teams through them, you'll give each team member confidence that they will always be seen and heard by both their leader and their colleagues.

This chapter addresses a range of important themes that influence leadership, including multigenerational dynamics, cultural agility, and fostering team cohesion. As you navigate these themes, it's inevitable that certain challenges, or stumbling blocks, will arise, particularly when leading diverse, multicultural teams. To effectively lead through these complexities, it's essential to anticipate and address the barriers that can hinder progress. Following are key stumbling blocks and practical strategies that align with the core themes of leadership, cultural shifts, and multigenerational collaboration, designed to help you overcome obstacles while building stronger, more cohesive teams.

 ## Stumbling Blocks and Strategies to Overcome Them

1. Differing Communication Styles

Stumbling Block: Miscommunication often occurs when different generations operate based on their distinct cultural contexts and communication styles.

For example, seasoned employees might prefer face-to-face conversations, and younger employees might be more comfortable with digital messaging platforms. This can lead to misunderstandings, and unmet expectations, and might even erode trust among team members.

Strategy to Overcome: Leaders need to establish clear communication protocols that bridge generational gaps. This includes offering training on effective communication tools and encouraging mutual respect for different styles. Leaders should encourage employees to articulate their preferences for communication and ensure that all voices, across generations, are heard. Create opportunities for both in-person and digital communication channels, providing flexibility for team members to engage in the ways they feel most comfortable.

2. Lack of Flexibility

Stumbling Block: Many leaders are accustomed to leading in a specific way and might resist adapting to the new needs of a multigenerational workforce or remote work environments. This rigidity can lead to disengagement, especially among younger team members who might expect more autonomy and less hierarchy.

Strategy to Overcome: Leaders need to adopt situational leadership, becoming "situational heroes," as mentioned in the chapter. This involves tailoring leadership styles to fit the needs of each individual or team and embracing agility. Leaders should focus on emotional intelligence, demonstrating adaptability in their decision-making, communication, and management approaches. Empowering team members through autonomy and flexible leadership will promote inclusivity and cohesion.

3. Tradition

Stumbling Block: Implementing cultural shifts in organizations can be met with resistance, especially when employees feel attached to established practices. This can hinder the integration of new approaches needed to foster innovation, inclusivity, and a dynamic work environment.

Strategy to Overcome: Leaders must first assess the current cultural landscape and then introduce SHIFTS in a way that connects deeply with the values of the organization. Engage teams in a process of collective cultural transformation by focusing on shared stories, rituals, and practices that everyone can rally around. Use storytelling and examples like The Oberoi's culture of service excellence to illustrate the benefits of intentional cultural change. Create spaces for open dialogue and allow people to share their experiences as cultural migrants, helping them transition smoothly to new organizational norms.

4. Lack of Interpersonal Connection

Stumbling Block: Remote work environments can lead to feelings of isolation and a lack of personal connection, especially when team members are spread across different time zones or cultures. This can negatively affect team morale and productivity if left unaddressed.

Strategy to Overcome: Reframe remote teams as digital campuses with their own set of rituals and systems for engagement. Leaders should prioritize creating strong, consistent virtual touchpoints, such as regular check-ins, virtual coffee breaks, and team-building activities, to foster cohesion. Leaders should also embrace technology that promotes not just efficiency but connectivity, ensuring team members feel part of a cohesive unit despite physical distance.

5. Differences in Values

Stumbling Block: Different generations might have varied expectations for work-life balance, career advancement, and performance metrics. Older generations might expect loyalty and long hours, and younger generations might prioritize flexibility and results over time spent in the office.

Strategy to Overcome: Leaders must clearly define success metrics based on productivity and outcomes rather than hours worked. Provide opportunities for mentorship across generations (speed mentoring), which allows both younger and older team members to learn from each other. Additionally, create a culture of flexibility by offering different paths for professional growth and performance evaluation, depending on the needs and aspirations of team members across age groups.

It's crucial to remember that first impressions rarely capture the full picture; much like an old book, people and situations can hold timeless wisdom and fresh insights when we take the time to understand them. As leaders, we must be intentional about extending the benefit of the doubt to others and encourage our teams to do the same. This builds a culture of trust, empathy, and inclusion, reinforcing that although we might come from different generations, cultures, or backgrounds, we are still united by our shared humanity. Throughout this chapter, we've explored how critical it is to navigate multigenerational and cultural SHIFTS, and how these experiences not only enrich our teams but also strengthen our organizations. When we see teams thrive across these divides, it's important to highlight and celebrate those successes, showing how they contribute to the broader organizational culture. These moments set the stage for the next phase of transformation, leading into the global SHIFTS we'll explore in Chapter 7. As we've discussed with each SHIFTS model step – from Seeing and Hearing and Insights to Formulating and Transforming – these changes are preparing us for larger, more impactful shifts on a global scale. The world is in the midst of major transformations, and understanding how to lead through these SHIFTS will be pivotal for both your organization and society as a whole. Prepare for what's to come – your world is about to shift in extraordinary ways.

Chapter 7

Leadership SHIFTS (Global and Cultural)

Global Perspectives in Leadership: Understanding Cultural SHIFTS

In an era defined by rapid globalization and cultural convergence, the landscape of leadership is undergoing profound transformations. The need for leaders who can navigate and adapt to these shifts has never been more critical. Chapter 7 explores these much wider leadership SHIFTS, focusing on how global and cultural changes demand a new kind of leadership – one that is culturally agile, aware, and adaptable.

As the world becomes increasingly interconnected, leaders are required to operate across diverse cultural landscapes. This chapter explores the importance of cultural awareness and adaptability as essential components of effective global leadership. Understanding and respecting cultural differences are not just niceties; they are strategic imperatives for leaders who seek to inspire, influence, and succeed on a global stage.

We will explore strategies for leading across cultures, addressing the challenges and opportunities that arise from cultural shifts. Leaders must learn to blend their vision with cultural intelligence, creating an environment where diverse teams can thrive. The SHIFTS model will serve as a guide, helping leaders to anticipate, respond to, and leverage cultural changes to foster growth and innovation within their organizations.

Ultimately, this chapter emphasizes that in our globalized world, leadership is not just about directing others; it is about understanding the cultural contexts in which leadership occurs. By mastering the art of cultural agility, leaders can not only navigate the complexities of the modern world but also lead with empathy, inclusivity, and effectiveness across cultural boundaries.

I've discovered a straightforward and practical way that the SHIFTS model in this book can be applied to the transformation of nations and our world. Remember, whatever you consistently and intentionally See and Hear will enter your subconscious mind, enabling you to reach new Insights and Formulate novel approaches that can Transform your daily experience into one of great Success. Just as this works on a personal level and in a corporate setting, the SHIFTS model has the potential to bring lasting, systemic change to a world in desperate need of trans-formational leaders.

Leaders with the courage to adopt this approach can lever-age the SHIFTS model to transform national values and cultures, and ultimately, national economies. We need transformational leaders that can change the mind of a nation.

When you stop to look at it, everything is connected. Con-nectivity is the air we breathe. And in this always-connected world, cultures blend. They are fluid. Our cultures have person-ality, just like you have a personality. No matter the geographi-cal area, culture boils down to the distinct personality of the region, serving as the common thread that binds a group of individuals into a collective humanity. To grasp a better under-standing, it's wise to start with the power of vision and its appli-cation in our leadership SHIFTS.

Class Is in Session, and Today's Subject Is Vision

There is a class I teach in Nigeria every year for our Daystar Leadership Academy (DLA) called "National Development." Even though I speak to adult audiences all over the world, it is thrilling for me every time I teach this class. I anticipate it months ahead with great excitement. Why? Because this class is designed for teenagers, usually ages 13–19. It's relatable to youth and developing minds, and it creates remarkable ideas, brainstorming, and tremendous excitement. It's organic in origin, well researched, fact-based, timely, and topical. And it eventually becomes experiential, because the students are asked to shift their mindsets and elevate all they think they understand about their country and their community's environment. In other words, I ask them how they will apply what they have learned.

I start the class by welcoming everyone and get right into revealing data that shows the negative effects of underdevelopment in various countries, specifically in our African nation. I focus on the high levels of illiteracy, high infant and maternal mortality rates, high levels of extreme poverty, and low life expectancy. This data sets the stage for understanding the long-term impact possible through global SHIFTS in underdeveloped countries and brings home the hard-hitting reality such transformation could have on student's lives, their families, and their future families.

When addressing the class, I approach these issues with strength and confidence, two traits important for young people to witness in action. I strongly convey, "There is nothing good about the underdevelopment of a nation." I also point out that many of the factors holding nations back from developing further have to do with their political evolution and educational systems, whereas others are steeped in cultural ideals that have been shaped by a variety of belief systems and generational influences. I go on to explore the cultural factors that influence national development and the factors that shape culture itself. This is when I make a case for change – urgent change. Apathy is unacceptable. The oppositive of love is not hate. It's apathy. When you are apathetic, it's the beginning of demise around you because you simply do not care any longer. People perish in the name of apathy. The only way things can change is when leaders implement vision through strong opinions, not indifference. This takes guts, especially in places where people are persecuted for their ideas or their disagreement with leadership. I want my students to walk among the brave with the courage to act when they see a need. I teach them that there's a torch for human excellence, and ask them, "Will you choose to receive the torch and shed light on things that are uncomfortable?" The only way to go deep within is to ask, "Am I leading for the greater good . . . something bigger than me?" "Do I behave from a heart filled with service and good intention, or am I out for number one – me?"

I ask my students to make a list of ways they feel they elevate humanity. Yes, of course they are young, but we are a collective consciousness, one humanity shifting forward for the greater good of everyone. Selfishness does not register here, and we are never too young to begin thinking beyond ourselves.

This resonates with teenagers because this is a time when some might act selfishly or think they really can't make a difference, especially at this age. But that's not true. When I share with them that they can make the necessary SHIFTS and create a new life story and live it out loud, the energy becomes palpable. The process model in this book is the example. You can be general and noncommittal, or you can be generous and declare your goals and their outcomes. The latter works best.

At this juncture, the mood in the class often becomes somber in the face of data that is, frankly, quite depressing. I go on to explain how we can create change and shift our mindsets by having a vision of our nation that enables us to see and imagine a developing economy. This is the target. This is the goal we aim for – a clear impression of the possibilities, with specific timelines for our goals and a plan to get there. Suddenly, the mood in the class starts to change. To make my point, I play a video for the class that shows various cities in Nigeria and their infrastructure (such as schools, hospitals, and train stations), comparing their current state to the way they could look one day, in 25–30 years. It's a glimpse into the future – their future. It's beautiful and hopeful. Often, the video causes loud applause, enthusiastic shouting, and a lot of chatting between the teens, followed by serious and thought-provoking discussion. It clearly hits a nerve. Every time I teach this class, the response is the same again and again, year after year. This "National Development" class is designed to shape young minds in a positive way. My organization offers this program every summer. It's something I look forward to facilitating whenever possible. I know its impact. I know how it gets the wheels in these children's heads turning.

Facilitating this class is one of my very favorites because of the raw enthusiasm the teenagers display in response to transforming nations. They get a sharp look into the future of their nation. They begin to feel their power. They start shifting paradigms and see possibilities they've never seen or discussed in a group before. In other countries, like the United States, these conversations start very young, but not in underdeveloped countries, like certain African nations, and others.

And that is certainly a shame, because who needs to embrace the power of transformational thinking more than cultures saddled with the gloomy data sets I begin class by discussing? And who is more ready to embrace the SHIFTS model than the young? It's certainly much easier to instill these ideas early, before culture and time and the pressures of adult life have created false beliefs and routines that must be deprogrammed before true growth can begin.

Some of the factors I discuss with the class are the things that shape a group's beliefs and behavior to create culture. These areas provide opportunities for us to leverage the SHIFTS model to create change. These factors include education versus ignorance, prevailing ideas about prosperity, the reward system in society and personal growth motivation, social welfare policies, religion, the media, and entertainment. There are other factors, of course, but I like to focus on these seven key areas that teens are typically eager to explore and discuss.

The SHIFTS model enables us to start chunking down each area. How you choose to expand and modify the content in your own discussions is up to you as a leader. I'll help you get started.

Education Versus Ignorance

The SHIFTS model is applied day in and day out at all educational institutions. Students See and Hear what is taught consistently. Next, they reflect on what they are taught to gain Insight as they apply what they learn. At higher levels of education, students See and Hear consistently for several years as they Formulate their life plan, Transforming themselves into doctors, lawyers, engineers, psychologists, or other professional titles on their way to ultimate Success.

On the flip side, ignorance and lack of confidence also shape beliefs and ultimately culture. They leave room for dangerous beliefs that rest on unverifiable myths. Ignorance creates a lack of awareness about how the world works. This stunts creativity and progress. More often than not, ignorance amplifies existing fears, causing people to become defenders of the very traditions that hamper progress. This is a lot to take in. It's frightening.

I was shocked the day one of my protégés shared what he saw on television some years ago. There had been air crashes back-to-back in Nigeria, and a local preacher's response was to begin warning his members against flying in aircraft. He spoke in one of the local languages, explaining that the manufacturers and builders of aircraft create the shell. He followed up by suggesting that the aircraft manufacturers put witchcraft power into the airplanes to make them fly. Someone reading this probably feels scandalized by such backward thinking. I felt this, too. How could someone think this way, let alone teach this? Here's the message: Ignorance is deadly to human potential at any level. This teacher was shaping the minds of his followers and stoking fear with unverifiable myths. The idea by itself is crushing and the ongoing outcomes are devastatingly unimaginable, yet ignorance exists in every generation and continues to shape vulnerable groups, especially the disenfranchised, poverty stricken, and fearful. They become the prey. It's of the utmost importance that SHIFTS take place, one baby step at a time.

Education plays a significant role in national development. Former prime minister of Singapore, Lee Kuan Yew, stated in his book, *From Third World to First*, that it took him time to see the obvious, that talent is a country's most precious asset, more valuable than anything tangible.[1] He described how a large proportion of Singapore's elite are graduates of Oxford and Cambridge. There is a famous quote from the former South African president and freedom fighter Nelson Mandela: "Education is the most powerful weapon you can use to change the world."[2] This might further underscore what I shared previously in this book. Knowledge is not power. What you do with knowledge – the *application* of knowledge – is your greatest power.

Leaders that will take our nations to their next levels in development need to be intentional in building educational institutions that help individuals to discover their unique strengths and help them to become innovators, challenging the status quo and creating solutions to their personal challenges and those of their organizations and nations. This is the way to cultivate citizens that build fast-developing economies. Educational systems in underperforming economies are usually only allowed to pass down dogmas and to produce conformists. They are usually also underfunded, with funds diverted to infrastructure that make corruption easy.[3]

Prevailing Ideas About Prosperity

Whenever I ask the young people in my classes for the quickest way to become rich in Nigeria, they mention politics and internet fraud ahead of other avenues for earning income. This is instructive as well as alarming. It doesn't matter how much teaching we do in schools or preaching we do in religious houses, people will always do whatever they have to do to survive. The instinct for survival is the strongest. Whatever people do repeatedly to earn an income, whether it is legitimate or not, becomes part of the culture in which they reside. This suggests that poverty has become part of the culture in some communities and nations to such a degree that it's assumed that the honest will always live in poverty, and the only way out is to embrace corruption. It's just accepted. Lifting people out of poverty should go beyond putting money in people's pockets. What's needed is mind SHIFTS and with that, the shifting of core values, and ultimately, the ways people earn income. Creating multiple visible avenues for people to create wealth *legitimately* can influence people's beliefs and behaviors.

For example, it is relatively easy to access credit to own a home with a good credit score and a good income in some countries, but this is only available for the elite in others. The need for shelter is basic. Making it easy to own a home can multiply avenues for earning income legitimately and lower the desperation to earn money through illegal or corrupt means. Many professionals earn income from the construction of a building and distributing wealth. At the end, the value remains in the building, and the owner can leverage that value as it increases with time. This is a subtle but powerful way to shift mindsets in a nation. Basic real estate opportunities can multiply exponentially, even within fluctuating economic times.

Also, it might be difficult to build a thriving tourism industry without value for recreation, vacationing, and hospitality. Some of the most underdeveloped communities and countries do not have a culture of vacationing because the struggle for mere survival is endless, leaving no time or resources for leisure. Studies show consistently that working without resting results in burnout and limits creativity and productivity. Here's an interesting metaphor. Scientists refer to the earth's sun as mediocre, in comparison to the billions of other stars. Though it's the brightest in our sky, and crucial for continued life on our planet, it's actually quite average. Supernovas burn bigger and brighter. They also burn out. Giant-size stars are not usually around long enough for their planetary systems to become hospitable for life to exist. But even though our sun might be astrologically quite common, it sustains life on earth. Stars like our sun burn slowly but shine brightly. Supernovas explode before reaching the same longevity. You might know people like this, too. They're called *flash in the pans*. Unlike these supernovas, which burn out before accomplishing anything of lasting worth, transformational leaders need to shape minds and hearts for the long haul. This means intentionally valuing concepts like rest, vacationing, tourism, and taking a break to appreciate life. They should not be seen as luxury for only the rich, but as investments to enhance creativity and productivity. This is a mindset. This is how SHIFTS are made at the cultural level. Just as Nike and I hung up a picture of our dream home and car, global leaders must constantly hold a picture of a nation's dream life in front of those they serve.

In addition, a community or country that will prosper needs to produce good-quality products for export. Exporting raw natural resources does not create much wealth for a nation because it is not competitive. Refining and manufacturing such resources into high-value products earns higher income. To do this, there must be a collective value for excellence. This requires a collective mind shift. Poor people often haven't been taught the concept of opportunity cost, leading them to focus merely on how much it would cost to achieve excellence, instead of what it would cost *not* to achieve it. Another metaphor is the difference between valuing price and cost. Let's say you want to buy a coffee maker. You buy the cheapest one available instead of paying $40 more for a better-quality product. The cheap coffee maker works for a few months and then breaks down. So, you buy another, then another. Soon you've spent far more than you had to, because you opted for lower-quality items instead of a quality, lasting product that you deserved to own in the first place.

This mindset results in missed opportunities as we lose ground to competition. Excellence is the achievement of good quality in an unusual degree. Whatever we spend to get good quality should not just be seen as an expense; it should be seen as an investment. This is the difference between asking "What is the price?" or "What will this cost me if I choose something lesser?" In most circumstances our money, our quality investment, will come back to serve us. Excellence attracts excellent resources, and it is the duty of a leader to convince their constituents that they deserve a SHIFT to a life in which they don't settle for low quality.

Helping people to understand the untapped potential in the way they earn and spend their money will shift mindsets, values, and culture to unleash the prosperity that lies trapped in their old ways of seeing.

The Reward System in Society and Personal Growth Motivation

People tend to do more and accomplish more when they are recognized and rewarded. The brain releases dopamine when we are recognized for a job well done. It then craves a repeat of the pleasurable feeling this creates. Transformational leaders create mindset SHIFTS and behavior SHIFTS by tweaking the reward systems for their groups. What is recognized communicates what a group of people values strongly and helps build nations.

There are three distinct types of motivation. Leaders often try to influence employee motivation, in some combination of these three ways:

1. Fear
2. Tangible incentives and rewards
3. Personal growth and opportunity

All these points motivate for a different reasons, which leads to patterns in their use. Fear motivation, for example, usually peaks when the economy gets sluggish, or when there are more qualified workers than jobs available. When people are motivated by fear, they're usually not trying to *get* something. Instead, they're trying to *avoid* something like pain or loss or embarrassment. Does fear motivation work? Yes, but only for a short period of time. It doesn't last. Fear motivation also leads to resentment and anger, often causing sabotage and disloyalty in the workplace.

Incentive and rewards motivation, however, can be a very good thing. People respond to being acknowledged and appreciated. But there is a catch here for leaders to be aware of. What happens after the reward is received? The potential trap can be the employee always wanting to be rewarded to do any specific task. So, leaders might find themselves trying to come up with different rewards so that performance does not slide back to the minimum. The carrot must keep getting bigger and bigger. In fact, we know that tasks performed merely for extrinsic rewards like this will always diminish over time because the reward comes to be expected as part of the status quo.

What I have found to work well is to blend the rewards concept with personal growth opportunity. When you give people a chance to excel and grow, you not only reward them but also you help them to feel more capable – both in the task at hand in their general ability to move toward the life they want. Motivation that ties to intrinsic rewards like this are very powerful, and often less financially costly than the "carrots" they'll eventually devalue anyway. It's human nature to look out for ourselves, and this combination of extrinsic rewards and personal growth opportunity is truly genuine and appreciated in the long haul.

Shifting Mindsets to Better Performance

Leaders cannot manage people like they manage budgets. Budgets can be viewed merely as numbers on a spreadsheet, but dealing with people always means managing relationships. These relationships you build will always influence what people are motivated to do. Essentially, you don't actually motivate *people* – you influence and shift what they're motivated to *do*. People will always move in the direction they believe to be in their best interests. So, pay attention to things that will have the most positive effect. It's this approach that helps build nations and confident teams.

> Leaders refer to intrinsic and extrinsic motivators. But in fact, motivation really is just intrinsic. It's something within every person. What we call extrinsic motivation is composed of things that influence our intrinsic motivational behaviors.

In underdeveloped nations especially, if you really want to influence people's desire to get on board and get moving with your plan, you must uncover their unique reasons for doing things. Whatever you're attempting must be presented in a way that makes the personal value proposition clear to them. For example, SHIFTing a nation's value set is going to be immensely difficult and complicated, especially at the start. But if we begin today, imagine the world we'll get to share with our children and grandchildren! The earlier you start this process, the better, like we do with teens at DLA. It's a start.

Social Welfare Policies

I had a conversation with some friends in the United Kingdom that helped me appreciate the value of social policies in shaping people's behavior, and it absorbed my attention for quite some time afterward. In this discussion, we began by talking about the high level of taxes paid in a wide variety of Western economies, relative to lower tax rates in many developing economies.

Even though most people do not enjoy paying taxes, it's widely known that there's often a connection between the taxes being paid and the quality of things like security, for instance. The insight that emerged from this conversation was driven by the weekly stipend that the UK government gives legal residents who are unemployed. This stipend goes to the purchase of groceries, lowering the desperation for survival that often drives up violent crime rates. During the conversation, someone proposed that we needed to make a choice. We could get comfortable with paying taxes and being able to drive in the evenings alone or walk our neighborhoods late at night without the fear of being attacked by criminals. Or we could pay lower taxes, and eventually have to move out of the country, as victimization by robbers and other crimes skyrocketed. It's a real dilemma no matter where you live, work, and raise a family. Seeking the balance of money and safety, taxes and crimes, lifestyles, and awareness is difficult, and each culture must find the equilibrium point that best serves its people.

Therefore, the SHIFTS model is not always going to work or apply everywhere. SHIFTS might not be effective in the face of extreme hunger, deprivation, or displacement. Transformational leaders who seek to shift minds need to address the most basic needs in their communities first and foremost. This is a larger topic – probably larger than this book – but it bears acknowledgment, which might lead to conversations that will begin closing the gaps between society's haves and have nots.

Religion

People worldwide visit religious institutions regularly, attend rituals and services, and listen to presentations that range far and wide within many belief systems around the planet. These practices exist from the most lavish of settings to the most remote jungle locations. Religion is bigger than its location. It is a mindset as well as a powerful platform that can be leveraged to create mind shifts, generation after generation. Religion shapes beliefs, values, and cultures. Conversely, culture also shapes religion. Every generation comes with its own list of questions, debates, and new models for cultural beliefs, rites and rituals, fresh perspectives, and a desire to build and create new ways to worship, interpret, and initiate religious and spiritual practices.

In fact, embracing this feedback loop between culture and religion might provide discussion points that can drive home the SHIFTS model. Just as every religion on earth periodically goes through periods of reevaluation, by finding new ways to connect with and affect people far removed from their origin, we can embrace the sort of SHIFTS that can bring prosperity to our nations in a way that doesn't discount or diminish the valuable contributions religion makes to the culture of a people.

The Richest Source of Values

Lawrence Harrison and Samuel Huntington assert in their book, *Culture Matters: How Values Shape Human Progress,* that religion has been the richest source of values throughout human history. Leaders in the religious space need to be intentional about the information that is disseminated constantly, bearing in mind the mindsets and values they form in the minds of individuals, and ultimately, the cultures they form in communities and nations.

For example, Russia's war with Ukraine, like many wars, is partly rooted in religion, which provides the undertone for the political dimension.[4] Samuel Huntington argues in his book, *The Clash of Civilizations and the Remaking of World Order,* that the world's major civilizations are based on cultural differences that have persisted for centuries and that these civilizations were largely shaped by religious traditions that are still powerful today.[5] He asserts that future political conflict will occur along these cultural divisions. The question is: Will we leverage religion to promote peace or conflict? And will we leverage religion to cultivate individuals who are catalysts for innovative thinking and economic progress, lifting everyone's quality of life, or will we produce conformists, sustaining age-old conflicts and slowing economic progress? The possibilities for meaningful SHIFTS are endless.

In this globalized world, leaders are increasingly required to navigate and respect religious diversity. Understanding and appreciating different religious perspectives can enhance a leader's ability to connect with people from various backgrounds.

Developing self-leadership involves cultivating intrinsic motivations and beneficial habits that align with one's values, including the respect for diverse religious beliefs.

Intrinsic motivation, rooted in genuine curiosity and empathy, enables leaders to engage with people of different faiths without prejudice. By practicing what we preach – such as inclusivity, respect, and humility – we set a powerful example for others. This self-leadership not only helps in personal growth but also in building a cohesive and respectful work environment.

Religion often influences the values and ethics of individuals and communities. Being mindful of this influence is crucial for leaders who aim to bridge age and culture gaps. These gaps can sometimes lead to misunderstandings and conflicts, particularly in a multicultural team. By acknowledging and addressing these differences, leaders can create an inclusive environment where everyone feels valued.

For example, understanding religious holidays and practices can help in planning work schedules and celebrations in a way that respects everyone's beliefs. This mindfulness not only fosters a positive work culture but also boosts morale and productivity. By working toward eliminating these gaps, leaders can ensure that all team members feel seen and respected, regardless of their religious background.

In today's interconnected world, leaders often find themselves leading teams spread across different countries and cultures. Making your presence felt, even from a distance, requires cultural agility and sensitivity to the religious and cultural contexts of your team members. Hiring for talent involves not only recognizing professional skills but also appreciating the diverse cultural and religious perspectives that individuals bring to the table.

Transparency is key to navigating these complexities. Being open about the importance of respecting diverse religious beliefs and practices can set a positive tone for the organization. This transparency fosters an environment of trust, where team members feel comfortable expressing their religious identities. By integrating these practices into your leadership style, you not only lead more effectively but also inspire your team to do the same. You're actually elevating your leadership styles.

As discussed in the previous chapters, the Six Steps to Transformational Leadership – See, Hear, Insight, Formulate, Transform, Succeed – offer a framework for creating positive mind shifts. When applied to the context of religious diversity, these steps can guide leaders in becoming more inclusive and respectful.

Religion is a significant factor in shaping beliefs, behaviors, and ultimately, culture. As leaders, we can leverage the SHIFTS model to create positive change. By fostering an environment of respect and understanding, we can help bridge tribal, cultural, and generational divides and promote social cohesion. This approach not only enhances our leadership capabilities but also enriches the lives of those we lead, closing a wide variety of communication gaps. As you continue to develop your leadership skills, remember that the changes you wish to see in the world start with yourself. Embrace the diversity around you and use it as a source of strength and inspiration in your leadership journey.

The Media

There will always be those who profit from the existing systems and structures, which means that anyone attempting meaningful change is going to draw attention. What do we do when we find ourselves or our organization in the crosshairs of a media storm?

I had what most people would consider a dream meeting with a celebrity many years ago. Yes, I was starstruck, but the point is that I saw it as a rare opportunity to ask a question that had been on my mind for a long time. There was an eye-catching headline about this person in the media almost every week, and they weren't positive. They were more like news scoops that were published by tabloids to sell publications. I seized the opportunity and asked if the things I had been reading about him were true. He said, "My brother, the way you read them is the way I get to read them, too. Most of them are not true." That discussion was a paradigm shifter for me. I wasn't well known then and had no idea the way such things work. The media just has the air of believability around it. They say it. We are to believe it. One of my friends calls most media stories manufactured train wrecks. I can understand why.

When You're in the Eye of the Media Storm

Since then, I've had my fair share of what I call media storms. At one time, a gentleman began coming by our office every day. This was some years ago. He insisted he had to see me and refused to give our office staff a hint of his subject matter or why he wanted to see me. He claimed to be a journalism professional but without specificity to his credentials.

He eventually threatened that he was privy to an inside story within our organization and wanted to give me an opportunity to state my side. This clearly sent up red flags. Something was off about his approach, and I smelled blackmail. I refused to see him. He published his unofficial story, and it went viral, but it had a short shelf life because it was untrue and based on lies.

All these years later, little has changed in certain media venues or tabloids. There is even greater incentive for such actions these days with the monetization of social media platforms and other outlets. This press attack against me was a wake-up call for our entire organization on the power of the media to try and shape public opinion or attack innocent, hardworking individuals who have an established celebrity or persona around them. This unethical behavior unfortunately shapes narratives, influences public opinion, and can even affect a company's bottom line. Media is a practical demonstration of the power of the SHIFTS model, because it presents what people See and Hear consistently, and it often has an implicit interest in protecting the existing establishment, which can stymie change at the cultural level.

This experience taught me that in our interconnected world, where news spreads at the speed of a tweet, leaders must navigate the media landscape with caution and strategy. The media, in all its forms, is a powerful tool that can either uplift or undermine, depending on how it is engaged. Understanding and leveraging this power has since become a critical aspect of my leadership approach.

In today's globalized digital world, media literacy is an essential skill for leaders. Developing self-leadership in this context means cultivating a critical and informed perspective on the media content we consume and produce. It's about understanding the motivations behind media messages, recognizing biases, and discerning between credible sources and misinformation.

Leaders must be adept at navigating both traditional and new media platforms. This involves being mindful of the information shared about the organization or nation and its leadership, and the narratives being constructed around them. By practicing transparency and authenticity in communications, leaders can build trust with their audience, both internally and externally. This self-awareness and media literacy are vital for maintaining a positive public image, effectively managing crises when they arise, and communicating efficiently at the scale that can bring about global change.

Without doubt, leaders and countries can leverage the media to sell compelling visions for their organizations and individual nations. It can be an amazing attribute. Traditional and social media can also be leveraged for formal and informal education. This way, the media can be leveraged to shift mindsets, shape values, and build the kind of culture that produces healthy economic development. For everything positive, there will always be a negative. It's your choice to elevate yourself or degrade yourself. How we discern the media's influence, use our good judgment and common sense, and choose carefully what we read, listen to, and watch will continue to transform our knowledge and how we choose to share and apply the knowledge we acquire. With the advent of artificial intelligence designed for mass consumption, the ways information gets produced and disseminated globally will proliferate even further. Although that can be scary, I like to envision all the positive that could come from these new media tools.

Entertainment

Any Nigerian old enough to have watched the final soccer match between Nigeria and Argentina at the 1996 Olympics is likely to still remember the experience. Nigeria won the match 3–2, and in that instant a nation with over 250 ethnic groups and languages became one in celebration. Let that sink in. It's extraordinary. I couldn't help but think about the power of entertainment to transcend borders, influence perceptions, and spark meaningful conversations. This experience reinforced my understanding that entertainment is not just a source of amusement but a potent tool for cultural exchange and social change. Entertainment is very effective for employing the SHIFTS model, because it provides content for people to See and Hear content consistently. It is effective in getting such content into the subconscious mind, because it usually evokes strong emotions.

Entertainment can be very effective for formal and informal education. The term *edutainment* refers to programs that blend fun and learning at the same time. This might take the form of games, movies, toys, television programs, and so on. Leaders can leverage these platforms to shape minds, values, and, ultimately, the behaviors that enable the achievement of their corporate or national visions. In addition, so much of this is easily available and even free in many cases. Selection of the information is the hardest part.

Entertainment fosters intercultural understanding. In today's interconnected world, entertainment has become a critical medium through which cultural narratives are shared and understood globally. Movies, music, television shows, and digital content serve as cultural bridges, offering audiences glimpses into lives and experiences different from their own. Remember my daughter's friend who learned English, not from a tutor or teacher, but from simply absorbing American movies? This global exchange enriches our understanding of the world and fosters empathy by highlighting both the diversity and commonalities of human experiences.

Entertainment shapes our perceptions of different cultures and societies. It plays a significant role in forming our worldview, often before we have the opportunity to experience these cultures firsthand. As leaders, understanding the impact of these cultural narratives is essential. It enables us to appreciate the nuances of different cultural perspectives and to approach global leadership with greater sensitivity and awareness.

Entertainment is a powerful tool that can influence beliefs, behaviors, and social norms. Developing self-leadership in the context of entertainment involves cultivating a critical and conscious approach to the media we consume. It means being aware of the messages conveyed through various forms of entertainment and understanding their potential impact on our values and behaviors.

Leaders must also be mindful of the content their organizations produce or endorse. In a world where entertainment and branding often intersect, it's crucial to align entertainment content with the organization's values and mission. This alignment helps build a consistent and authentic brand image, fostering trust and loyalty among audiences.

Furthermore, leaders should encourage critical consumption among their teams and audiences. This involves promoting media literacy, helping people discern between entertainment that uplifts and educates and that which perpetuates stereotypes or harmful narratives. By fostering a culture of critical consumption, leaders can contribute to a more informed and conscientious society. In an age of misinformation and pervasive digital content, fostering media literacy within the organization empowers teams to critically evaluate the media they consume and produce. This skill is vital for preventing the spread of harmful narratives and ensuring that the organization's content contributes positively to public discourse.

The global entertainment landscape is constantly evolving, influenced by technological advancements and shifting consumer preferences. With the rise of streaming platforms and social media, entertainment is more accessible and diverse than ever before. This democratization of content has empowered creators from all corners of the world to share their stories with global audiences.

Leaders must navigate these trends thoughtfully. Embracing global entertainment means recognizing and supporting diverse voices and stories. It involves being open to new genres, formats, and cultural expressions that might challenge traditional norms or offer fresh perspectives. By doing so, leaders can foster a more inclusive and dynamic entertainment environment, reflecting the rich tapestry of human experiences Supporting diverse voices is not only a moral imperative but also a strategic advantage. By embracing a wide range of perspectives, organizations can tap into new markets, appeal to a broader audience, and drive innovation in content creation.

Moreover, understanding global entertainment trends helps leaders anticipate changes in audience preferences and stay ahead in a competitive market. It enables organizations to adapt their content strategies, ensuring they remain relevant and engaging to diverse audiences. This adaptability is key to thriving in the ever-changing entertainment industry. Leaders who actively monitor and respond to global entertainment trends can position their organizations as industry leaders. By anticipating shifts in audience preferences, they can craft forward-thinking strategies that keep their brand relevant and ahead of competitors.

Entertainment is more than just a pastime; it is a powerful force that shapes our worldviews and cultural landscapes. As leaders, we have the opportunity to harness this power for good. By fostering a diverse and inclusive entertainment environment, promoting critical consumption, and supporting meaningful content, we can contribute to a more empathetic and informed global society.

In the age of globalization, the stories we tell and consume matter more than ever. They shape our understanding of each other and influence the social and cultural norms we live by. As you continue your leadership journey, consider the role of entertainment in your strategies. Embrace its potential to inspire, educate, and unite. Through thoughtful engagement with the entertainment landscape, we can lead with empathy, understanding, and a commitment to positive change. In this dynamic landscape, adaptability is not just a survival tactic – it is the foundation of long-term success. Leaders who embrace change and innovate in their content strategies will not only thrive but also will set new benchmarks for the industry, leading their organizations into a prosperous future.

Partnerships Across Borders – Make the Shift to Global Leadership

Francis Olubambi, the West and Central Africa coordinator for the Global Leadership Network, organizers of the renowned Global Leadership Summit, shared an idea with me several years ago. He and his team wanted a suitable venue to host the Global Leadership Summit in Nigeria and they felt that our church facilities would be appropriate. We agreed and hosted the summit. That began a partnership between us that continues to bring positive impact to thousands of emerging leaders. My team and I are very proud of this accomplishment.

When I was invited to speak at the summit in Chicago, the organizing team requested that I visit their office in Chicago on one of my trips to the United States. Of course, I said yes. It was necessary to close some cultural gaps in our shared understanding and ensure that our teams remained sensitive to each other's differences and opinions. As I entered the meeting room, I was greeted with warm smiles and a gesture of respect that immediately set a positive tone. Over the course of the meeting, I realized that building a partnership across cultural differences required not just a sound business proposition but also sensitivity and a genuine willingness to understand and respect the nuances of another's experiences.

This partnership was an eye-opener. It underscored the importance of cultural intelligence and adaptability in forming successful cross-cultural partnerships. It also taught me that becoming a global leader involves more than just expanding business operations; it requires building bridges of trust and mutual respect across diverse cultural landscapes. My presentation was translated into many languages and was broadcast at events in scores of countries across all continents. This has created opportunities for me to speak at conferences in many countries. At the same time, the local version of the conference, which began at our location in Nigeria, has spread to over 100 locations. It has been a productive partnership.

In an increasingly interconnected world, the ability to navigate cultural differences is a crucial skill for global leaders. Cultural intelligence, or the ability to understand and adapt to different cultural contexts, is essential for forging strong international partnerships. It involves recognizing and respecting the values, communication styles, and business practices of other cultures.

Leaders with high cultural intelligence are adept at reading social cues and adjusting their behavior accordingly. This skill is invaluable in negotiations, where understanding the subtleties of another culture can make the difference between a successful deal and a missed opportunity. Moreover, cultural intelligence fosters empathy, enabling leaders to build deeper, more authentic relationships with partners and stakeholders across the globe.

Developing cultural intelligence starts with self-awareness. Leaders must recognize their own cultural biases and be open to learning about others. This openness, combined with active listening and observation, can help leaders navigate the complexities of cross-cultural interactions and build partnerships based on mutual respect and understanding.

Global markets present both opportunities and challenges for businesses. Understanding local market dynamics, consumer behavior, and regulatory environments is crucial for success. Leaders must be well versed in these factors to make informed decisions and develop strategies that resonate with local audiences.

For example, a marketing campaign that works in one region might not translate well to another due to cultural differences or local regulations. Leaders must be willing to adapt their strategies and approaches to suit the unique characteristics of each market. This adaptability is key to building a strong international presence and fostering long-term partnerships.

Moreover, navigating global markets requires an understanding of economic and political trends. Leaders must stay informed about global events and their potential impact on international business operations. This awareness enables them to anticipate challenges, mitigate risks, and seize opportunities as they arise.

Trust is the cornerstone of any successful partnership, and this is especially true for cross-border collaborations. Building trust requires consistent and transparent communication, as well as a commitment to honoring agreements and respecting cultural differences.

Leaders must be mindful of how their actions and decisions are perceived by their international partners. This includes being sensitive to different communication styles and expectations about punctuality, decision-making processes, and conflict resolution. Demonstrating a genuine respect for these differences can help build a strong foundation of trust and mutual respect.

Furthermore, leaders should strive to create a win-win scenario in their partnerships. This means being fair and equitable in negotiations and ensuring that both parties benefit from the collaboration. By fostering a sense of shared goals and mutual benefit, leaders can build lasting and fruitful partnerships across borders.

Technology plays a crucial role in enabling global collaboration. With the rise of digital communication tools, virtual meetings, and cloud-based platforms, it's easier than ever to connect with partners and teams around the world. Leaders must leverage these technologies to facilitate seamless communication and coordination across time zones and geographies.

However, effective use of technology also requires an understanding of the digital landscape in different regions. For instance, the popularity, use, and even legality of social media platforms can vary widely between countries. Leaders should be aware of these differences and tailor their digital strategies accordingly to engage with local audiences effectively.

Additionally, leaders should promote digital literacy and ensure that their teams are equipped to use these tools efficiently. This includes providing training and support to help team members navigate different technologies and platforms. By fostering a digitally savvy workforce, leaders can enhance global collaboration and drive business success.

Becoming a global leader requires more than just expanding business operations across borders. It involves cultivating cultural intelligence, building trust, and leveraging technology to connect with partners and teams worldwide. As leaders navigate this complex landscape, they must remain adaptable, open-minded, and committed to fostering genuine, respectful relationships.

In the end, the true measure of a global leader is not just in the number of international partnerships formed but in the depth, and quality of these relationships. By embracing diversity, promoting inclusivity, and leading with empathy and integrity, leaders can not only drive business success but also contribute to a more connected and collaborative global community. As you continue your journey toward global leadership, remember that the most impactful partnerships are those built on a foundation of trust, mutual respect, and a shared vision for the future.

Let me make a final point before moving on. One of the most important lessons I've learned is the value of empathy in global leadership. I recall my visit to Togo to speak at the local version of the Global Leadership Summit. As I stood on the stage, I sensed a gap between the audience and me. It seemed to me that they could not possibly imagine that I knew what it felt like to experience deprivation. Despite the language barrier, I felt a deep connection with the people there, who were eager to share their stories and learn from me. I shifted my presentation to include personal stories of how bad things were for my family when my dad's business had no income. I described how our family discussed the importance of carefully pushing toothpaste out of the tube slowly so it could last, eventually even using a scissors to cut the tube so we could clean out the last bit of paste. The crowd became animated, cheering and laughing at an experience they knew all too well – and now understood was an experience we shared. This moment taught me that, regardless of cultural differences, the fundamental human desire to connect, learn, grow, and meet basic needs is universal.

As a leader, it's crucial to put yourself in others' shoes, to listen and learn with an open heart. It's not about imposing your way of doing things, but about finding common ground and building on shared values. This empathy not only fosters deeper relationships but also opens new possibilities for collaboration and innovation.

In conclusion, my experiences and insights have underscored the critical roles of empathy, cultural intelligence, and collaboration in global leadership. These are all critical and important emotional intelligences. As we navigate an increasingly interconnected world, these qualities are essential for building meaningful partnerships and driving sustainable success. By embracing these principles and intelligences, we can become true global leaders, capable of making a positive impact across borders and cultures. SHIFTS are almost always guaranteed when we do this.

Best-selling author and keynote speaker Brendon Burchard, author of *The Motivation Manifesto*, said, "A society that lacks good people willing to speak against evil or low standards can only devolve into darkness and mediocrity."[6] This is an excellent point. Regardless of the nation we lead in, how do we get people to make SHIFTS that lead them to a higher standard? When I speak on this subject to government officials and CEOs in companies around the world, I explain that my work in this area is not just a class, or course, or executive retreat. It is a movement. Together we can rise to higher standards. Together we can gain support and understanding. And together we can be virtuous and not only transform mindsets but elevate the leadership standard of courage and greatness. The moment has come to shift mindsets globally and with confidence and pride. The fact is, there's not more time, because the time is now.

The Interdependence of Nations

No nation is self-sufficient. Each nation has to depend on others in various ways. Industries in some countries depend on raw materials or parts from other countries. Against this backdrop, conflicts between nations are detrimental to human progress. Yet countries continue to increase their military arsenals in response to perceived threats from their neighbors. We are beginning to see countries move against those that colonized them because they desire greater autonomy in the management of their resources. The belief is widespread that there is a deliberate manipulation of the world order and, sometimes, interference in local politics to give some countries access to cheap resources to keep their industries running. It is important for leaders to be conscious that we all need to move our world toward peace, cooperation, and interdependence, which will in turn help us to overcome the global challenges of poverty, illiteracy, disease, climate change, and so on, one step at a time. As global leaders, we have the innate power to leverage the SHIFTS model to move toward achieving these objectives. But the SHIFTS must start from within first.

The rapid improvements in information and communication technologies have accelerated interconnectedness among individuals, organizations, and nations. This has created many opportunities in the exchange of financial and human capital, along with improvements in manufacturing processes. However, there are challenges in spite of these positive developments.

There is trade imbalance because of lack of capacity in some countries.

In my article for the World Economic Forum on Africa, I assert that globalization does not appear to be hastening Africa's development, and that the problem is rooted in political structures and leadership culture.[7] I advised that aid given to countries on the continent would not improve people's lives because they would be consumed by the elite, and that development partners should focus first on working with local partners to enhance leadership development, especially in the large population of youth who want a better future for their continent. This is just an example of how we can identify and begin to solve root problems.

I remain hopeful and confident that together we can cooperate across borders to make our world better and create bigger and more powerful positive SHIFTS that will elevate us all.

Everyone has influence. Influence rises and falls at all levels. Life exists outside of our own backyard. A leader's ability to influence does not depend on their position in the company. Here are two exercises to examine with your own group. How can you expand on these exercises to fit your specific context and culture?

EXERCISE **Exercise: Make a Point of Mentoring**

Objective: To express to your team the importance of establishing a culture of mentoring and provide them with some launch points that will make the process begin smoothly and intentionally.

INSTRUCTIONS

Formalize Your Intentions: Begin with an all-hands meeting in which you express your intention to formalize the process of mentoring. Mentoring is always happening somewhere in your organization, but it's often an informal, ad hoc process that is left for employees to navigate on their own. As the leader, it's your job to set clear guidelines and expectations for the mentoring process. (And, yes, part of this should include you letting the employees know that you, too, are involved in a mentoring relationship as you strive to become the best leader you can for their benefit.)

Establish Connections: Have each employee list two to three members of the company whom they don't work with each day but that they feel could nonetheless offer them valuable advice in some area – even if it's something outside the workplace, like personal finance or parenting. Then have them use the other side of the same card to list another set of two to three members of the company that they feel they could *offer* help to. When they're done, you'll have a giant web of potential connections that you can use to establish a network of formal mentoring relationships.

Provide a Framework: Don't just announce the mentor pairing and throw them to the wolves. Many people, especially those new to the mentoring process, need some structure to feel comfortable. Mentoring templates are readily available online. For a general template, you might point them to something like this simple set of guidelines and templates, or you could take the time to customize something for your specific needs.

(continued)

(continued)

Evaluate, Tweak, and Iterate: Set a date to reconvene and evaluate the program's progress, which will give you the opportunity to discover what worked well, and what can be improved.

Our Culture Is Our Business: Especially in regions of the world that suffer from high poverty and low citizen satisfaction, the business community has a unique opportunity to improve the lives of those around them – simply by finding ways to apply the principles of successful business to the lives of the citizens around them. To do this, have team members create their own business case for a change they'd like to bring to their community.

 Exercise: Making Impact in the Community

Objective: To make members of your organization to be sensitive to gaps in the culture outside your organization.

INSTRUCTIONS

Choose Your Change: Break employees up into small groups and have them brainstorm the friction points that create pain or inconvenience in the daily lives of the community outside their business. Each group should come up with two to three solvable problems. After the lists are generated, post them all, and ask employees to put themselves into small groups of four to five dedicated to solving one of the problems.

Run It Like a Business: Ask each group: If our company tasked you with solving this problem, what business case would you make that would be compelling enough for management to immediately to want to hire a team to carry out your idea? At minimum, they should include an outline of the problem, the steps necessary for its solution, an estimate of the budget and headcount it would require, and a timeline for completion.

Execute the Vision: When business cases have been turned in, you now possess something powerful: a set of plans to effect tangible change in the world outside your company walls. You could put it to a company vote or you could select the best plan yourself – either way, you now have at least one plan that emerged from the bottom up that will affect your immediate community, has a clear plan for execution, and enjoys significant internal buy-in. String together a few of these in a row, and your group can become a model for others, creating a ripple effect that could potentially affect an entire culture.

STUMBLING BLOCKS Stumbling Blocks and How to Avoid Them

1. Avoid the "My Way or the Highway" Mentality

Stumbling Block: Insisting on one way of doing things can alienate others and stifle innovation.

Strategy to Overcome: Recognize that leadership in a global context demands flexibility. Embrace diverse perspectives as opportunities for growth and creativity. By valuing different approaches, you not only enhance team dynamics but also foster a more inclusive and adaptive leadership style.

2. Keep Pace with Technological Advancements

Stumbling Block: In today's fast-paced world, technological stagnation can be a significant barrier to effective leadership.

Strategy to Overcome: Continually seek out new tools and platforms that can enhance communication, collaboration, and efficiency within your team. Staying technologically current is not just about adopting the latest trends but also about ensuring that your team is equipped to thrive in a digital-first world.

3. Embrace and Navigate Cultural Differences

Stumbling Block: Cultural differences are not obstacles but opportunities to deepen understanding and collaboration. However, disagreements can lead to friction if not handled with care.

Strategy to Overcome: Cultivate an environment where diverse cultural perspectives are respected and used as a foundation for innovative problem-solving. Learning to navigate and reconcile these differences is key to successful global leadership.

4. Stay Informed and Attuned to Your Environment

Stumbling Block: Ignoring or filtering out critical information can lead to missed opportunities and significant leadership missteps.

Strategy to Overcome: Stay attuned to the flow of information within your organization and the broader market. Regularly seek feedback, stay informed about global trends, and be proactive in addressing emerging challenges. Vigilance and continuous learning are essential to maintaining relevance and effectiveness in leadership.

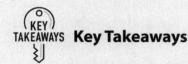

Key Takeaways

Effective global leadership is grounded in empathy and cultural intelligence. Understanding and connecting with people from diverse backgrounds not only strengthens relationships but also drives organizational success in a multicultural world. Leaders who cultivate these qualities can inspire trust, foster inclusivity, and lead with greater impact.

At the heart of global leadership lies the principle that, despite our differences, we are united by shared human values. Embracing this unity while respecting cultural diversity is key to building a more cohesive and collaborative global community. Leaders must lead with the understanding that every culture contributes to the rich tapestry of humanity.

True global leadership transcends geographical expansion. It requires a deep commitment to

(continued)

Leadership SHIFTS (Global and Cultural)

(continued)

understanding cultural nuances, fostering trust across diverse teams, and strategically leveraging technology to bridge gaps. Leaders who succeed in the global arena do so by integrating these elements into a cohesive strategy that aligns with both organizational goals and global realities.

Transformational leadership is about more than just implementing change – it's about inspiring and empowering others to reach their full potential. Develop a clear plan to transition into this leadership style, focusing on how you can motivate your team, drive innovation, and create a vision that resonates on a global scale. This shift will position you as a leader who not only manages but truly transforms.

In global leadership, perception is everything. Cultural sensitivity and awareness are critical to ensuring that your actions and decisions are perceived positively across different cultural contexts. Be proactive in understanding how your leadership style and decisions are viewed by international partners, and adjust accordingly to maintain strong, respectful, and productive relationships.

We began the book's journey at a simple table, in a simple restaurant, as Nike and I stared out a simple window and allowed ourselves to dream of the SHIFTS we'd like to see in our lives and the lives of our children. Those SHIFTS enabled us to build the life we now enjoy, and will continue to reverberate through generations in our children's lives and beyond.

Additionally, the SHIFTS mindset has rippled outward through space, affecting our business, enabling us to expand and grow into the organization we lead today – one that has true global impact in countries around the world. My hope is that this book will plant the seeds that grow into more stories like this, enabling the SHIFTS mindset to move from something that has external impact in various places into the internal heart of entire countries. That is when SHIFTS can truly become a global phenomenon.

Conclusion: The SHIFTS Impact

I want to sincerely thank you for allowing me to join you on your journey to transforming your mindset and elevating your leadership. I hope you've enjoyed our journey together through the SHIFTS approach, but more important, I hope you've found value in it.

When I sat down to write this book, I originally thought about how these lessons could help my teams do better and be better. But then I thought bigger. These lessons are not just for my team and my leaders. They are for any team and every leader. It is my hope that you can see yourself in the examples of my personal experiences and formulate your own growth as you move forward, wherever you live and whatever your culture, environment, age, status, or dream for a better tomorrow.

The fact is that none of these ideas are complicated, but the surest truths rarely are. As C. S. Lewis wrote to a friend shortly before the beginning of World War II:

> The process of living seems to consist of coming to realize truths so ancient and simple that, if stated, they sound like barren platitudes. They cannot sound otherwise to those who have not had the relevant experience; that is why there is no teaching of such truths possible, and every generation starts from scratch.[1]

Like Lewis, I have found truth to be remarkably uncomplicated, yet often incredibly difficult to put into practice.

The simple truths you've learned here are the Six Steps to Transform Your Mindset and Elevate Your Leadership, along with how to use them to author your own success story. You're the only author of your story. No one else. Previous chapters you have written or journaled may influence future ones, but looking within yourself and practicing self-leadership can help you determine if you are indeed writing the correct story or if you need to make "edits" to SHIFT your mind, thoughts, actions, habits, and behaviors.

By applying the Six Steps, I believe you can overcome anything if your head and heart are in the right place. You cultivate self-awareness and embrace a willingness to adapt to any circumstance. Once you experience a personal shift, you can take the opportunity to help others move in a direction that is beneficial toward their goals as well as the goals you share. Your leadership can become a gift to others.

The SHIFTS model is a simple acronym I developed to help me in that regard. At first, it was a simple mnemonic device to help me frame the changes I hoped to see in my own life and the life of my family. However, as it took root and began to reshape me from the inside out, I realized it could have powerful impact on the people around me, the businesses and ministries I managed, and even the world itself.

Today, we've seen over 52,000 people graduate from our leadership school, and I can access three million minds on social media. The SHIFTS process has served me well, and my hope and prayer is that it will serve you likewise.

SHIFTing Never Stops

Or at least it shouldn't. Most people pick up books like this one because they're seeking help to deal with an immediate,

Conclusion: The SHIFTS Impact

pressing issue. Perhaps you felt stagnated in your career, or didn't know how to get one started. Perhaps you've found yourself in a position of leadership that threatens to overwhelm you, and you're dealing with a bit of impostor syndrome. Perhaps you've found yourself in personal debt, and you're looking for the tools to manage impulses and value long-term discipline over short-term benefit.

And the SHIFTS model can help with any of those things. But it doesn't have to stop there. SHIFTS is an ongoing process, one that can be repeated and replicated again and again, in every arena of life and business, across multiple contexts. In fact, that's when it works best; implementing it successfully to bring about the first positive change in your life gives you the practice and confidence to ensure that the next iteration will be more successful, over and over again, until you look around in wonder like I did one day, realizing that the life I had dreamed of years ago as I looked through a restaurant window with my wife was now the world I walked around in each day.

Invention and Reinvention

Imagine being addicted to cocaine – at age 13. Imagine being arrested nearly 20 times and spending 45 days in jail – all before you were old enough to vote. Imagine looking at the rest of your life, envisioning nothing but an endless chain of bad decisions, pain, and despair.

However, imagine the respect of your peers and fans. Imagine wealth beyond your wildest dreams. Imagine having the resources to build a charity that distributes over $12 million to those in need and provides thousands of children with a summer camp experience they would never otherwise be able to afford.

Imagine that those were *both* your story. Because the two previous paragraphs each describe Academy Award nominee Mark Wahlberg.

But the most fascinating part of Mark Wahlberg's story (at least to me) isn't the journey from Boston street tough to actor, philanthropist, and entrepreneur. It's the way station in the middle of his story.

Because before he was Mark Wahlberg, the brooding star of Martin Scorsese's Academy Award–winning film *The Departed*, working alongside film icons like Jack Nicholson, he was a rapper with the stage name Marky Mark. And in 1991, Marky Mark and the Funky Bunch hit the Billboard Top 100 with their dance single "Good Vibrations" – a song that would eventually sell over a million copies, and often heard in athletic stadiums to this day.

Wahlberg, the youngest of nine children, had experienced a difficult youth and a tempestuous relationship with the law, so you might think this success would be enough. A single song, recorded with a few friends, would completely SHIFT his financial future, his social status, and the rest of his material life.

To be sure, the early indications were that material change was the only kind Wahlberg was experiencing. Even after "Good Vibrations" made him a household name, his behavior did not seem much improved: in 1992, he fractured a neighbor's jaw in a physical altercation.

Still, Wahlberg kept SHIFTing. From music, he moved into advertising, becoming a Calvin Klein model in shoots featured worldwide. From modeling, he began exploring the potential of an acting career, where he truly hit his stride. His second film, *The Basketball Diaries*, was an adaptation of poet Jim Carroll's autobiography; this role garnered the attention of the industry, leading to steady work and eventually making him the world's highest-paid actor in 2017.

And, somewhere along the way, as he was SHIFTing his external life from street hoodlum to musician to model to actor to global icon, Wahlberg was undergoing some internal SHIFTS as well. Today, he's a husband who has never been divorced, a father to four children, and an active member of his faith community who describes his faith as the most important part of his life. These internal SHIFTS eventually led him to establish a foundation dedicated to supporting underprivileged children.

Though I've never met Wahlberg, I can't help but think that he is a sort of walking symbol of the SHIFTS model and its iterative approach to continuous improvement. When many people from his background would have been happy merely to have their material needs met in a way that ensured they'd never know lack again, something in Wahlberg led him to a continual process of ongoing growth, going through invention and reinventions that completely SHIFTed him, time and again, into the man he is today.

 Exercise: Where Have You Been? Where Are You Going?

Apps like Timehop, or the Memories feature on Facebook, are interesting because they afford us the opportunity to regularly look back at who we once were. Each day, we can check that date for years past, pulling up the photos and thoughts we posted in our past. This exercise is sort of a Timehop for your SHIFTS process.

Objective: Developing Your SHIFTS Plan

(continued)

Conclusion: The SHIFTS Impact

(continued)

INSTRUCTIONS

Memorialize: Take a moment to flip back and review all the other exercises from the book, considering the realizations you've come to, the important decisions you've made, and the things you plan to change to bring your life in line with your vision. Write them down someplace you'll be able to find them later, like a document saved to your computer desktop or a bedside journal. Don't concern yourself with format, spelling, or grammar; just get everything down in stream-of-consciousness style for as long as you can keep the words flowing.

Chart Your Course: Reading back over your list, focus on the decisions you've made for change. For each one, write down three next steps – one to be taken tomorrow, one to be taken within week, and one to be taken within one month.

Hold Yourself Accountable: Most email services can schedule emails in the future. Right now, schedule an email to yourself for one month from today. That email simply needs to read "How are your SHIFTS going?" Each day for the next month, you'll see the document on your desktop or the journal you used to write in, and at the end of the month, you'll get an email from yourself reminding you of the promises that were made by the version of you who existed a month ago. This process can be repeated each month, or six months, or once a year as you get better at managing the intervals.

Stumbling Block and Strategy to Overcome It

Momentum Drift

Stumbling Block: Momentum is easy to maintain and hard to revive. Objects in motion tend to stay in motion, and objects at rest tend to stay at rest. Even the most diligent among us occasionally give way to complacency; it's the human condition. Especially when things begin to go right for a while – in these moments, it's easy to forget that our current situation is the result of hard work, and we fall prey to the assumption that the benefits we've accrued will keep coming our way forever.

Strategy to Overcome: First of all, if you took this chapter's exercise to heart, you're already on the right track, because you'll be getting an email in just a short while that will force you to confront the vision you've laid out for yourself. Whether the intervening month has brought you closer or further from that vision, you'll have the opportunity to immediately schedule another email, giving yourself another opportunity.

Beyond that, though, you need accountability outside yourself. A spouse, friend, or trusted colleague should also be in on the vision, so take the time to explain to them why you read this book, what your vision entails, and what you're doing about it. And, most important, ask them to check in with you periodically to ask how it's going, and tell them up front that they have permission to speak freely and bluntly on the topic. Often, we'll work harder to affect the opinions of those we respect than we will for our own vision. Bringing someone else in the loop leverages this tendency to give your SHIFTS the maximum chance for success.

What I Hope You've Learned

You learned that your mindset and your personal values are important, but application is critical to your success. You cannot merely think your way to success. It takes action to set the wheels of transformation in motion. Those who embrace transformation and open-mindedness as guiding principles can transcend the status quo and achieve unimaginable possibilities.

You learned that when you step past tired old practices and apply transformational SHIFTS with empathy and kindness to your teams and organizations, you can realize high levels of trust and loyalty. It is these visionary mind SHIFTS that can nurture an environment where creativity thrives, and boundaries are continually pushed.

You learned that standing on your personal values is at the heart of transformative leadership. At their most basic, values guide your thoughts and beliefs. Organizations also have values. When you align personal and team values with your organizational values, everyone can row in the same direction. There are no limits to the possibilities you can realize.

You learned that talent spans generations and cultures. Everyone brings a background and a lived experience to the table, and with it, a unique worldview. Leverage this knowledge to build a rock-solid team that does bold and innovative things.

You learned that leaders could lead from anywhere in the world, across time zones and cultures. By hiring for talent and leveraging the collective strength of your team, you can experience the true innovation that can spring only from a diversity of thoughts, beliefs, cultures, and experiences.

You learned that crushing barriers and pushing boundaries all boil down to transformational mind SHIFTS. Elevating your leadership means thinking in a way that you have not ever considered before. It is setting a new vision for yourself, your life, your organization, your nation, or your world, and acting on it. It is taking a risk on being vulnerable, and being willing to learn from what does not work out. You have transformed your leadership into a beacon that lights the way for others to follow. And together you can move forward, achieving success.

Look how far you have come. I hope you'll give yourself credit. I'm confident that you have made major SHIFTS while reading this book. Ralph Waldo Emerson said, *Do not go where the path may lead; go instead where there is no path and leave a trail.* SHIFTS is a book that helps leaders to leave a trail for their followers. The end of this book is the start of something greater. I'd like to hear from you. Send me your stories of success and heartfelt input on social media. Visit me at one of my worldwide events and introduce yourself. I'd be honored to meet you. There's no specific code for successful leadership. We are all a collective consciousness of new and exciting ideas that are making SHIFTS in the many ways we do business, lead, communicate, and build long-lasting relationships.

I trust that the guidance I have provided can inspire and excite you for the journey ahead. I truly believe in your potential to become a leader who in turn can inspire and guide others to their own success.

Key Takeaways

The SHIFTS model is not intended as a quick fix to a temporary problem, though it can be used as such. I've intended for you to receive it as a lifelong leadership tool, whether you're leading just yourself or a team of 100.

It's pretty unlikely that you're a juvenile delinquent with dreams of a Calvin Klein contract and a Martin Scorsese film. But you're holding this book in your hands, which means there is a tension in your life; something about where you are has led you to the truth that it's not where you want to be, and I believe with all my heart that you don't have to stay here. But it's stronger than mere belief: I know it.

I know SHIFTS works because I've lived it, and know it because I've led it in others.

May all your SHIFTS be successful, and may they never stop happening. I look forward to seeing all that you'll accomplish as you take what you've learned and begin leading with vision, adaptability, and deep purpose.

So long for now, and I hope to be seeing you soon.
Sam Adeyemi

SHIFTS Notes

Introduction

1. Cho, Y. D. (1979). *The Fourth Dimension*. Bridge Logos Publishers.

Chapter 1

1. Allen, J. (2022). *As a Man Thinketh*. Readers Library Classics.
2. Warren, R. (2002). *The Purpose Driven Life: What on Earth Am I Here For?* Zondervan.
3. Volf, M., Croasmun, M., & McAnnally-Linz, R. (2023). *Life Worth Living: A Guide to What Matters Most*. The Open Field.

Chapter 2

1. Alpuim, M., & Ehrenberg, K. (2023). Why Images Are So Powerful – And What Matters When Choosing Them. Bonn Institute (August 3). https://www.bonn-institute.org/en/news/psychology-in-journalism-5
2. TD Bank. (2016). https://www.prnewswire.com/news-releases/visualizing-goals-influences-financial-health-and-happiness-study-finds-300207028.html
3. Fazio, L. K., & Sherry, C. L. (2020). The Effect of Repetition on Truth Judgments Across Development. *Psychological Science*, 31(9), 1150–1160.
4. Ritchie, S. J., Bates, T. C., & Plomin, R. Does Learning to Read Improve Intelligence? A Longitudinal Multivariate Analysis in Identical Twins from Age 7 to 16. *Child Development*, 86(1), 23–36.

5. de Leeuw, R. N. H. & van der Laan, C. A. (2018). Helping Behavior in Disney Animated Movies and Children's Helping Behavior in the Netherlands. *Journal of Children and Media, 12*(2), 1–16.
6. Huesmann, L. R., Moise-Titus, J., Podolski, C.-L., & Eron, L. D. (2003). Longitudinal Relations Between Children's Exposure to TV Violence and Their Aggressive and Violent Behavior in Young Adulthood: 1977–1992. *Developmental Psychology, 39*(2), 201–221. 10.1037/0012-1649.39.2.201
7. Center for Disease Control. (2023). https://www.cdc.gov/childrensmentalhealth/data.html (retrieved July 22, 2024).
8. Center for Disease Control. (2022). https://www.cdc.gov/media/releases/2022/p0331-youth-mental-health-covid-19.html (retrieved July 22, 2024).
9. Twenge, J. M., & Campbell, W. K. (2018). Associations Between Screen Time and Lower Psychological Well-Being Among Children and Adolescents: Evidence from a Population-Based Study. *Preventive Medicine Reports, 12*, 271–283.
10. Grontved, A., Singhammer, J., et al. (2015). A Prospective Study of Screen Time in Adolescence and Depression Symptoms in Young Adulthood. *Preventive Medicine*; Volume *81*, pp. 108–113.
11. Maras, D., Flament, M. F., Froberg, K., Møller, N. C., Pan, A., Pfeiffer, K. A., & Kristensen, P. L. (2015). Screen Time Is Associated with Depression and Anxiety in Canadian Youth. *Preventive Medicine, 73,* 133–138.
12. Making Caring Common. (2023). On Edge: Understanding and Preventing Young Adults' Mental Health Challenges. https://mcc.gse.harvard.edu/reports/on-edge
13. Burkus, D. (2021). *Leading from Anywhere: The Essential Guide to Managing Remote Teams*. Mariner Books.
14. De Becker, G. (2021). *The Gift of Fear: Survival Signals That Protect Us from Violence*. Dell Publishing.
15. Jal, E. (2012). *See Me Mama*. Gatwitch Records.
16. Weinberg, M. K., & Joseph, D. (2016). If You're Happy and You Know It: Music Engagement and Subjective Wellbeing. *Psychology of Music, 45*(2).

17. Anderson, C. A., Carnagey, N. L., & Eubanks, J. (2003). Exposure to Violent Media: The Effects of Songs with Violent Lyrics on Aggressive Thoughts and Feelings. *Journal of Personality and Social Psychology, 84*(5), 960–971.
18. UNESCO. (2017). Out-of-School Children, Adolescents and Youth: Global Status and Trends. *Policy Paper 32/Fact Sheet 44.*
19. Tyndale House. (2006). Proverbs 13:20. *Holy Bible: New Living Translation.*
20. Adeyemi, S. (2022). *Dear Leader: Your Flagship Guide to Successful Leadership.* Amazon/KDP.

Chapter 3

1. Sawhney, M., & Khosla, S. (2014). Where to Look for Insight. *Harvard Business Review* (November).
2. Bailey, J. R., & Rehman, S. (2022). Don't Underestimate the Power of Self Reflection. *Harvard Business Review* (March).
3. Levitt, S. D. (2016). Heads or Tails: The Impact of a Coin Toss on Major Life Decisions and Subsequent Happiness. National Bureau of Economic Research. *Working Paper 22487* (August).
4. Hill, N. (2007). *Think and Grow Rich.* TarcherPerigee.

Chapter 4

1. Clear, J. (2018). *Atomic Habits.* Avery Publishing
2. Johnson, S. (2002). *Who Moved My Cheese.* Putnam.

Chapter 5

1. Parker, K., & Horowitz, J. M. (2022). Majority of Workers Who Quit a Job in 2021 Cite Low Pay, No Opportunities for Advancement, Feeling Disrespected. Pew Research Center (March 9). https://www.pewresearch.org/short-reads/2022/03/09/majority-of-workers-who-quit-a-job-in-2021-cite-low-pay-no-opportunities-for-advancement-feeling-disrespected/

2. Maxwell, J. (2022). *The 21 Irrefutable Laws of Leadership* (p. 70). HarperCollins Leadership.
3. Chand, S. (2023). *Turbo Leadership: Power Points for Maximum Performance*. Avail.
4. Squires, S. E., Smith, C. J., McDougall, L., & Yeack, W. R. (2003). *Arthur Andersen: Shifting Values, Unexpected Consequences* (pp. 82–83). FT Press.
5. Anwar, M. F., Danna, F. E., Ma, J. F., & Pitre, C. J. (2021). *Love as a Business Strategy: Resilience, Belonging and Success* (p. 32). Lioncrest Publishing.
6. Covey, S. R. (2013). *The 7 Habits of Highly Effective People: Powerful Lessons in Personal Change*. Simon & Schuster.
7. Michelli, J. A. (2008). *The New Gold Standard: 5 Leadership Principles for Creating a Legendary Customer Experience Courtesy of the Ritz-Carlton Hotel*. McGraw-Hill Education.

Chapter 6

1. Maxwell, J. C. (2007). *The 21 Irrefutable Laws of Leadership*. HarperCollins Leadership.
2. Buell, R. W., Raman, A., & Muthuram, V. (2015, January). Oberoi Hotels: Train Whistle in the Tiger Reserve. *Harvard Business School Case 615-043* (revised March 2015).
3. Toler, S., & Nelson, A. E. (1999). *The Five Star Church: Helping Your Church Provide the Highest Level of Service to God and His People*. Baker Publishing Group.
4. Orlowski, F. (2024). Cultivating a Culture of Well-Being: Investing in Employee Mental Health Fortifies Ethics. *CEP Magazine*.
5. Schein, E. H. (2010). *Organizational Culture and Leadership*. Jossey-Bass.
6. Biro, M. M. (2023). Hiring Gen Z Talent? Check Your Assumption at the Door. *Forbes* (July 21). https://www.forbes.com/sites/meghanbiro/2023/07/21/hiring-gen-z-talent-check-your-assumptions-at-the-door/
7. Pew Research Center. (2023). About a Third of U.S. Workers Who Can Work from Home Now Do So All the Time (March 30).

https://www.pewresearch.org/short-reads/2023/03/30/about-a-third-of-us-workers-who-can-work-from-home-do-so-all-the-time/

8. Schwantes, M. (2019). A New Study Reveals Why Working from Home Makes Employees More Productive (October 4). https://www.inc.com/marcel-schwantes/new-study-reveals-why-working-from-home-makes-workers-more-productive.html

9. Atlassian. (2020). Being Transparent Can Ensure Remote Success—Here's How to Achieve It (October 1). https://www.atlassian.com/blog/distributed-work/transparency-is-essential-to-remote-success

Chapter 7

1. Yew, L. K. (2000). *From First World to First* (p. 135). Harper Collins.

2. Mandela, N. (1990). Speech given at Madison Park High School Boston on June 23, 1990. Nelson Mandela Foundation Archive.

3. Harrison, L. E., & Huntington, S. P. (2000). *Culture Matters: How Values Shape Human Progress*. Basic Books. 3.

4. Burgess, J. P. (2022). Is Russia's War on Ukraine About Religion? *The Christian Century* (March 23). https://www.christiancentury.org/article/features/russia-s-war-ukraine-about-religion

5. Hungtington, S. (1996). *The Clash of Civilizations and the Remaking of World Order*. Simon & Schuster.

6. Burchard, B. (2014). *The Motivation Manifesto*. Hay House.

7. Adeyemi, S. (2017). Africa Doesn't Need Charity: It Needs Good Leadership. World Economic Forum. https://www.weforum.org/agenda/2017/05/africa-doesn-t-need-charity-it-needs-good-leadership/

Conclusion

1. Lewis, C. S. (2004). In W. Hooper (Ed.), *The Collected Letters of C. S. Lewis (Vol. II): Books, Broadcasts, and the War, 1931–1949* (pp. 256, 258). Harper.

Acknowledgments

I work and travel at a frenetic pace, and it would have been incredibly difficult to produce a work of high quality like this within a short time without the contributions made by highly talented people. I thank Anne Bruce, who played an undeniably major role, putting in a word for me with Wiley and coordinating the teams involved. I thank Jeanine Finelli and Phyllis Jask for making invaluable contributions, teaming up with Anne Bruce and me on the writing.

I am grateful to Cheryl Segura, my brilliant editor at Wiley. Cheryl teased the SHIFTS model out of me and provided support all the way to the release of the book. It was inspiring working with other brilliant professionals at Wiley. Sangeetha Suresh coordinated the project as managing editor. Others included Amanda Pyne and Laura Cooksley. Of course, it wasn't practical to meet all the Wiley staff and teams involved in this project, but I appreciate everyone.

Emily Nolan is a caring and highly experienced editor. She ensured that the SHIFTS message came through the writing with clarity, and for that, I am grateful. I thank Susan Geraghty for putting finishing touches to the manuscript with her exceptional editing skills. I also thank Michelle Nicholson, my publicist, who along with the management at Wasabi Publicity was very understanding and accommodating of my requests. Their excellent writer, Jay Adams, helped me to meet editorial deadlines with incredible speed. Thank you, Jay.

My profound appreciation to Dr. Taiwo Ojo and Dr. Toye Sobande, who were helpful with the initial research I needed to support the SHIFTS principles. My appreciation to other members of the Sam Adeyemi GLC, Inc. team, who showed creativity and excellence as my sounding boards at different stages, from creating the SHIFTS acronym, to researching the title, deciding on the cover design, transcribing audio notes, and planning the marketing. The team includes David Ayodele, Yemi Dokun, Boye Oloyede, Sophie Adeyemi, and David Adeyemi. A special thank you to those I call SHIFTS champions, who began to spread the word about this book even before I was done writing it.

I thank my children, Sophie, David, and Adora Adeyemi, for introducing brilliant and fresh perspectives to my work always. I appreciate your love and support. I am fortunate to enjoy the love, support, and talent for detail of my wife and sweetheart, Nike Adeyemi. Thank you for your love and support through our many SHIFTS.

About the Author

Dr. Sam Adeyemi is a global conference speaker, author, executive coach, strategic leadership expert, and minister who shifts mindsets so his audiences and clients can more clearly envision possibilities and then become those possibilities. He is the CEO of Sam Adeyemi GLC, Inc., which hosts the annual High Impact C-Suite Leadership Retreat, and is the founder and executive director of Daystar Leadership Academy (DLA). More than 52,000 alumni have graduated from DLA programs. Dr. Sam has more than three million social media followers and continues building a strong movement of high-impact leaders internationally. He's known for helping to shape the destinies of aspiring leaders and their families, while helping transform the organizations and nations they work in with his popular SHIFTS model. Dr. Adeyemi is the author of *Dear Leader: Your Flagship Guide to Successful Leadership.* He holds a master of arts in leadership studies and a doctorate in strategic leadership and has a background in engineering. He and his wife, Nike, founded Daystar Christian Centre and have three children. Visit and learn more about Sam and his books and programs at SamAdeyemi.com.

Unlock Your Next Level of Leadership

SHIFTS: FREE MASTERCLASS

Leadership | Transformation | Growth

The leadership journey you've been waiting for has arrived. Join Dr. Sam Adeyemi for a free masterclass and learn the powerful strategies he has developed over 30 years of leadership coaching, and take your place as a transformational leader.

Remember what Dr. Sam always says, "A shift in mindset can transform your entire life."

This masterclass includes:

- Deep dive into the SHIFTS blueprint

- Downloadable notes

- Lifetime access

Sign up now for free at https://shifts.samadeyemi.com/

SHIFTS

Don't just rewrite a new story,
live it out!

SEE	You are the sum of what you repeatedly See.
HEAR	You are the sum of what you repeatedly Hear.
INSIGHT	Your Insight and feelings anchor your beliefs about yourself and the world.
FORMULATE	Your belief system Formulates your decisions and creates habits.
TRANSFORM	Your decisions Transform your actions for making those big, bold moves!
SUCCEED	Your actions lead to Success. No, you're not dreaming!

Index

Page numbers followed by *f* refer to figures.

240

241

Index

244

Index